RESTORATIVE JUSTICE
IN THE
BOOK OF ROMANS

Dr. Maxwell Shimba

TABLE OF CONTENTS

Preface v

Introduction vii

Chapter 01 1

Understanding Restorative Justice in the Book of Romans 1

Chapter 02 12

Theology of Justice 12

Chapter 03 30

Paul's Perspective of Justice 30

Chapter 04 47

Sin and Its Consequences 47

Chapter 05 61

Redemption and Atonement 61

Chapter 06 77

Reconciliation 77

Chapter 07 91

Forgiveness and Repentance 91

Chapter 08 106

the Role of Community 106

Chapter 09 120

Restitution and Repair 120

Chapter 10 135

Practical Applications 135

Chapter 11 153

Challenges and Critiques 153

Chapter 12 173

Contepolary Relevance 173

Chapter 13 190

Restorative Justice in the Church 190

Chapter 14..210

Building a Restorative Society.......................................210

Chapter 15..230

Conclusion and Future Direction..................................230

PREFACE

Reconciliation and Restoration: Exploring the Teachings of Romans in Restorative Justice

In a world often marked by conflict, punishment, and division, the teachings of the Apostle Paul in the Book of Romans serve as a beacon of hope, offering profound insights into a different path—a path of reconciliation, healing, and restoration. This book, "Reconciliation and Restoration: Exploring the Teachings of Romans in Restorative Justice," embarks on a journey through the ancient yet ever-relevant wisdom found in the Book of Romans, unraveling the deep theological underpinnings that have the power to transform lives, communities, and even societies.

We live in a time where our understanding of justice is at a crossroads. Traditional punitive systems, while effective in some aspects, have not quelled the root causes of conflict and harm. It is within this context that restorative justice—a paradigm rooted in the idea of repairing harm and rebuilding relationships—gains prominence. And, as we delve into the core of this paradigm, we find the teachings of Romans shining with clarity and wisdom.

This book is a tapestry woven from the timeless teachings of Romans and the dynamic principles of restorative justice. We journey through the pages of Romans, guided by its teachings on justice, sin, redemption, reconciliation, and the central theme of faith in Christ. Each chapter meticulously examines these aspects and connects them to the evolving philosophy of restorative justice. Together, they paint a comprehensive picture of how the Book of

Romans serves as a theological cornerstone for this approach to justice.

In our exploration, we not only uncover the theological foundations but also bridge the gap between the sacred and the secular, applying these principles to real-world situations. We traverse the pathways of practical applications in the criminal justice system, educational institutions, and even within the Christian community, envisioning a world where restorative practices are woven into the fabric of society.

The chapters unfold the challenges and critiques that restorative justice faces, the role of faith communities in promoting these principles, and the potential for a society transformed through reconciliation and restoration. They culminate in a vision of a future where restorative justice is not merely a choice but an integral part of how we address wrongdoing and harm.

In the ever-changing landscape of justice and reconciliation, this book serves as a compass, guiding readers through the teachings of Romans, reflecting on their relevance to the challenges of our times, and charting a course towards a more compassionate, equitable, and reconciled world.

We invite you to journey with us through the teachings of Romans and the evolving landscape of restorative justice. Let these pages be your guide, your inspiration, and your source of wisdom as you embark on your quest for reconciliation and restoration.

With profound gratitude for your readership,

Dr. Maxwell Shimba

President

Shimba Institute for Restorative Justice

INTRODUCTION

The Book of Romans in the New Testament of the Bible primarily focuses on Christian theology and the teachings of the Apostle Paul. While the term "restorative justice" is a modern concept, there are elements in Romans that can be interpreted in alignment with the principles of restorative justice.

In Romans, there is an emphasis on reconciliation, forgiveness, and redemption. These concepts can be seen as aspects of restorative justice:

1. Reconciliation: Romans stresses the need for reconciliation, not only between humans but between humanity and God. Restorative justice also aims to reconcile those who have been harmed and those who have caused harm.

2. Forgiveness: The book discusses forgiveness as a central theme, emphasizing the idea of forgiving others as God has forgiven us. Restorative justice often involves forgiveness and the willingness to move beyond the harm caused.

3. Redemption and Atonement: Romans teaches about the redemption of sinners through faith in Jesus Christ and the atonement for sins. Restorative justice seeks to address and repair the harm caused by offenses, leading to the redemption of both the offender and the victim.

While the term "restorative justice" is not explicitly mentioned in Romans, the themes of reconciliation, forgiveness, and redemption align with the core principles of restorative justice. Restorative justice, in modern terms, involves addressing harm, repairing relationships, and promoting healing, and these concepts can find resonance in the teachings of Romans.

viii

DR. MAXWELL SHIMBA

CHAPTER 01

UNDERSTANDING RESTORATIVE JUSTICE IN THE BOOK OF ROMANS

In his profound exploration of theological concepts in the letter to the Romans, the Apostle Paul initiates his discourse with a visionary statement found in 1:16: "I am not ashamed of the gospel; for it is the power of God for salvation to everyone who has faith, to the Jew first and also to the Gentile. In the gospel, the justice of God is revealed through faith for faith."

Paul's reference to "the justice of God" encompasses a cosmic transformation, where the personal and societal realms undergo a unified and transformative divine intervention. This intervention, orchestrated by God, seeks to bring healing and restoration to all facets of creation. (For an in-depth exploration, see Marshall's work, "Beyond Retribution").

Crucially, Paul intricately connects "justice" with "salvation." In the biblical context, God's "justice" represents the divine work to mend brokenness – a concept akin to "restorative justice." Paul's perspective on God's "justice" aligns with a characteristic that leads to salvation, not punishment, even for God's adversaries (see Romans 5:1-11).

Paul proclaims that God's "justice" has now been "revealed." The term "revealed" (apokalypsis, the root of "apocalypse") often signifies a transformative and epoch-defining message from God. For Paul, this revelation conveys that, in Jesus, the kingdom of God has become manifest. Those who grasp this revelation experience a profound shift in their perception of the world.

In 1:17, Paul further emphasizes that the "just shall live by faithfulness." Throughout the letter to the Romans, it is reiterated that this faithfulness is most potently expressed in the unity between Jews and Gentiles, underscoring Paul's vision of a harmonious and inclusive faith community.

A deep exploration of restorative justice within the context of the Book of Romans involves delving into key passages and themes of the book to draw connections with the principles of restorative justice. Here, we'll explore some of these connections:

1. Reconciliation: Romans emphasize the need for reconciliation, both between individuals and between humanity and God. In restorative justice, reconciliation is a fundamental principle, seeking to repair broken relationships and promote harmony. The Book of Romans underscores the importance of reconciliation as a means to address the separation caused by sin.

2. Forgiveness: Romans highlights the idea of forgiveness as a central Christian virtue. It teaches that humans should forgive one another, just as God has forgiven them through Christ. This

aligns with restorative justice, which often involves the offender acknowledging their actions and the victim extending forgiveness as a step towards healing and restoration.

3. Repentance and Transformation: Romans describes the transformation of believers through faith in Christ. Restorative justice encourages offenders to take responsibility for their actions, express genuine remorse, and seek transformation. The Book of Romans supports the idea of personal transformation as a path to reconciliation and restoration.

4. Justice and Mercy: Romans discusses the balance between justice and mercy, particularly in relation to God's judgment. Restorative justice aims to balance accountability with a compassionate response to wrongdoing. It is about holding offenders accountable for their actions while also offering them an opportunity to make amends and rebuild their lives.

5. Community Engagement: The Book of Romans emphasizes the importance of the Christian community and its role in the lives of believers. Similarly, restorative justice often involves the community in the resolution process. Communities can play a vital role in providing support to victims and helping offenders reintegrate into society.

6. Restitution and Repair: Romans teaches about making amends for wrongdoing. Restorative justice often involves restitution, where offenders take concrete steps to repair the harm they caused. This may include compensating victims or engaging in community service.

A deep exploration of restorative justice in the context of Romans also involves considering the challenges and critiques of applying these principles within a Christian framework. Some may argue that restorative justice is incompatible with punitive justice, which the Bible also mentions. Addressing such challenges and seeking a balance is an essential part of this exploration.

Following this introduction, Paul delves into a critical issue. He dissects the dynamics that lead people from a rejection of truth to ingratitude, resulting in misplaced trust in created things and the subsequent spiral into uncontrollable desires, injustice, and violence. This unfolding dynamic embodies what Paul describes as "wrath," a divine response that involves God "giving them up" to a self-chosen path of spiritual deterioration.

In 1:17, we encounter the profound revelation of God's justice, a redemptive concept. However, in the subsequent verse, we witness the suppression of truth that paves the way for the "revelation" of God's wrath. Through "justice," individuals recognize created things as mere pointers to the Creator, not as false deities deserving of ultimate devotion. Such insight leads to life. Conversely, the alignment with "wrath" occurs when loyalty is directed toward created entities, resulting in the suppression of truth and a downward spiral into spiritual desolation.

God has embedded within creation itself guidelines that should lead to a state of "justice." Here, "justice" is linked to a fundamental attitude of gratitude toward life, fostering kindness, generosity, and the wholeness of relationships. Regrettably, many have not lived in this state of gratitude (1:22), leading to a prevalence of brokenness in human existence.

Individuals exchange their identity as God's children for "images" that resemble created things. This exchange prompts a shift from justice to wrath, from life to death. Paul emphatically asserts that this transition is not inevitable. God has revealed what humanity requires. As Paul explains, "What can be known about God is plain to them because God has shown it to them..., seen through the things he has made" (1:19-20). Nevertheless, when people trade "the glory of God" for images that mimic created things, their ability to discern God's revelation is lost.

In 1:28, Paul revisits the dynamic in which "God gives them up," this time to a "debased mind." Consequently, they are unable to perceive reality as it truly is. God's revelation of love becomes wrath to them instead of the life-affirming justice it is meant to be. Trusting in entities other than God clouds their capacity to think, perceive, and understand profoundly.

The progression towards injustice inexorably unfolds as people engage in the worship of "created things." This progression involves the suppression of truth (1:18), a refusal to honor and give thanks to God (1:21), the darkening of minds (1:21), the exchange of God's glory for lifeless images (1:23), being "given up" to degrading desires (1:24), the worship of created entities rather than the Creator (1:25), the indulgence in debasing passions (1:26), shameless acts (1:27), debased minds (1:28), culminating in profound injustice and violence (1:29-31).

A deep exploration of restorative justice within the context of the Book of Romans, with accompanying Bible verses, can be divided into several key themes:

1. Reconciliation and Peace:

Romans 5:1 - "Therefore, since we have been justified by faith, we have peace with God through our Lord Jesus Christ."

The concept of reconciliation and peace is central in Romans. Restorative justice seeks to restore peace and harmony between individuals, mirroring the reconciliation between humanity and God that the Book of Romans emphasizes.

2. Forgiveness and Grace:

Romans 3:23-24 - "For all have sinned and fall short of the glory of God, and all are justified freely by his grace through the redemption that came by Christ Jesus."

This verse underscores the idea that, just as God's grace forgives all who have sinned, restorative justice encourages the forgiveness of those who have wronged others. It emphasizes the transformative power of grace and forgiveness.

3. Transformation and Renewal:

Romans 12:2 - "Do not conform to the pattern of this world, but be transformed by the renewing of your mind."

Restorative justice aims at the transformation of offenders, seeking their renewal and reintegration into society. Romans speaks of the transformation brought about through faith in Christ, aligning with the restorative justice goal of personal growth and rehabilitation.

4. Justice and Mercy:

Romans 12:19 - "Do not take revenge, my dear friends, but leave room for God's wrath, for it is written: 'It is mine to avenge; I will repay,' says the Lord."

This verse highlights the balance between justice and mercy. Restorative justice seeks to address wrongdoing while showing mercy, allowing room for reconciliation and healing. The concept of God's ultimate judgment aligns with the idea of accountability in restorative justice.

5. Community Involvement:

Romans 12:4-5 - "For just as each of us has one body with many members, and these members do not all have the same function, so in Christ, we, though many, form one body, and each member belongs to all the others."

Romans emphasizes the interconnectedness of the Christian community. Similarly, restorative justice often involves the community in the resolution process. The concept of a supportive, interdependent community is essential in both contexts.

6. Restoration and Making Amends:

Romans 13:8 - "Let no debt remain outstanding, except the continuing debt to love one another, for whoever loves others has fulfilled the law."

Restorative justice often involves making amends, or restitution. Romans emphasizes the fulfillment of the law through love and highlights the importance of resolving debts, which can be seen as making amends for wrongs committed.

Incorporating these Bible verses, we see how the Book of Romans provides a scriptural foundation for restorative justice principles. The themes of reconciliation, forgiveness, transformation, justice, and community involvement found in Romans align with the principles of restorative justice, making a strong case for the application of restorative justice within a Christian framework.

Understanding restorative justice is important for several reasons:

1. A More Compassionate and Healing Approach: Restorative justice provides an alternative to punitive justice systems. It places a strong emphasis on repairing harm and promoting healing for both victims and offenders. Understanding this approach helps society move away from punitive measures that often perpetuate cycles of harm and instead opt for a more compassionate response.

2. Empowering Victims: Restorative justice prioritizes the needs and voices of victims. By understanding this approach, we acknowledge the importance of empowering victims to participate in the resolution process, allowing them to express their feelings and needs, and contributing to their sense of justice.

3. Accountability and Responsibility: Restorative justice encourages offenders to take responsibility for their actions. This accountability can lead to personal growth and rehabilitation. Understanding restorative justice recognizes that holding individuals accountable while offering them a chance for redemption can lead to a more just society.

4. Reconciliation and Community Building: In a world marked by conflict and division, restorative justice promotes reconciliation and community building. By understanding this approach, we recognize the potential for repairing damaged

relationships and fostering a sense of belonging and connectedness within communities.

5. Reducing Recidivism: Restorative justice has shown success in reducing re-offending rates. By addressing the root causes of criminal behavior and providing support for reintegration, it contributes to safer communities. Understanding this can lead to more effective criminal justice systems.

6. Aligning with Human Rights: Restorative justice aligns with many principles of human rights, including dignity, respect, and the right to be heard. This understanding reinforces the importance of respecting and upholding these rights within the justice system.

7. Modernizing Justice Systems: In the modern world, where issues such as mass incarceration and the high costs of punitive justice are becoming increasingly apparent, restorative justice offers an innovative and cost-effective approach. Understanding and implementing these principles can lead to more efficient and humane justice systems.

Hence, restorative justice is a significant concept in the modern world as it offers a more compassionate, healing, and effective approach to addressing harm and conflict. It emphasizes repairing harm, fostering reconciliation, and promoting healing for all parties involved, contributing to a more just and humane society.

The purpose of this book is to bridge the gap between the teachings of the Book of Romans and the principles of restorative justice. This exploration is of comprehensive importance for both theologians and those interested in restorative justice, as it seeks to harmonize the biblical teachings of Romans with modern concepts of justice and reconciliation.

Romans 1:16-17 - "For I am not ashamed of the gospel, because it is the power of God that brings salvation to everyone who believes: first to the Jew, then to the Gentile. For in the gospel the righteousness of God is revealed—a righteousness that is by faith from first to last, just as it is written: 'The righteous will live by faith.'"

This verse highlights the power of the gospel to bring salvation to all through faith. It serves as a foundation for the purpose of this book, aiming to reveal how the principles of restorative justice align with the righteousness of God.

Romans 15:4 - "For everything that was written in the past was written to teach us so that through the endurance taught in the Scriptures and the encouragement they provide we might have hope."

The teachings of Romans provide a rich source of wisdom and guidance. This book aims to show how these teachings can provide endurance and encouragement in the context of restorative justice, offering hope for those seeking a more compassionate and healing approach to justice.

Romans 12:18 - "If it is possible, as far as it depends on you, live at peace with everyone."

This verse emphasizes the importance of living in peace with others. The purpose of this book is to explore how restorative justice can contribute to this goal by fostering reconciliation and harmony in the face of wrongdoing.

Therefore, the purpose of this book is to connect the teachings of Romans with the principles of restorative justice, illustrating their compatibility and relevance. It holds significance for theologians by deepening their understanding of biblical concepts in a contemporary context. It is also crucial for those interested in restorative justice, as it offers insights into how biblical wisdom can inform and enrich modern approaches to justice and reconciliation.

CHAPTER 02

THEOLOGY OF JUSTICE

The Book of Romans in the New Testament of the Bible provides several theological foundations of justice:

1. God's Righteousness: Romans emphasize the righteousness of God as the ultimate standard of justice. The book teaches that God is perfectly just and that His justice is based on His character, which is inherently righteous and fair (Romans 3:26).

2. Justice and the Law: The Book of Romans discusses the relationship between justice and the Mosaic Law. It highlights that the law revealed God's standard of justice, but it also recognizes the limitations of the law in making individuals righteous. Instead, the law serves to reveal human sinfulness and the need for a savior (Romans 3:20).

Paul's concerns in 1:18-32 revolve around the perils of idolatry and the urgent need to break free from its enslaving grip. It is vital to recognize that accusing others of idolatry while failing to acknowledge one's own inclination to worship idols hinders the path to liberation. Therefore, the very actions of those who point fingers, often labeled as "judgers," are themselves manifestations of idolatry (2:1).

Even Paul himself, prior to his transformative encounter with Jesus, grappled with his own substitution of God with the rigid boundaries that defended a faith built on a perceived need for violent defense. Paul's "degrading passions" were not confined to the sexual realm but extended to the ideological, ultimately resulting in the same outcome—unjust practices and violence.

Upon encountering Jesus, Paul discovered a profound truth: violence invariably signifies a departure from truth. The very truth he believed he was upholding turned out to be a falsehood. The works of the law that he passionately defended were, in reality, rooted in idolatry. Paul realized that he had been as much of an idolater as those who held positions of power in the Roman Empire.

In 2:5, Paul refers to "God's just judgment" using the same terminology employed in 1:32, translated as "God's decree." The first group of idolaters understood this decree but chose to disregard it, thereby perpetuating their unjust conduct. The second group of idolaters will face the unveiling of God's just judgment "on the day of wrath." The injustices detailed in 1:29-31 and the judgment in 2:1-2 are similar in nature; both obscure individuals' perception of God's authentic justice. By rejecting the life-affirming justice of God, both categories of idolaters condemn themselves to experience God's justice in the form of wrath.

3. Justification by Faith: A central theme in Romans is the concept of justification by faith. This theological foundation is crucial for understanding justice in a Christian context. It teaches that individuals are declared righteous before God not by their own

works but through faith in Jesus Christ. This emphasis on faith as the means of righteousness aligns with the divine aspect of justice (Romans 3:21-24).

4. Justice and Mercy: Romans grapple with the balance between justice and mercy. It discusses how God's justice is harmonized with His mercy through the atoning sacrifice of Jesus Christ. This demonstrates that God's justice does not simply demand punishment but offers a way for humanity to be reconciled to Him through His grace (Romans 3:25).

5. Justice for All: The universality of salvation in Romans underscores a sense of justice for all people, regardless of their backgrounds. The book teaches that the gospel is for both Jews and Gentiles, emphasizing inclusivity in God's redemptive plan. This principle aligns with the notion of justice for all and equitable treatment (Romans 10:12).

6. Justice and Sin: Romans addresses the consequences of sin and the need for redemption. The book underscores the reality of human sinfulness and its separation from God. Understanding the gravity of sin is foundational to grasping the justice-seeking aspect of God's character and the need for restoration (Romans 3:23).

These theological foundations in Romans contribute to the Christian understanding of justice as rooted in God's righteousness, the need for faith for justification, and the harmonization of justice and mercy. They provide a framework for discussions of justice and reconciliation in a Christian context.

God's righteousness, as presented in the Book of Romans and throughout the Bible, is the concept that God is the ultimate standard of moral and ethical perfection. It serves as the foundation for understanding justice within the Christian theological framework. Romans emphasizes that God's righteousness is the basis for justice, and human justice should align with His character in the following ways:

1. Moral Perfection: God's righteousness signifies that He is entirely free from any moral flaw or imperfection. His character is marked by absolute goodness, holiness, and integrity. This moral perfection is the ideal standard against which all human actions and decisions are measured.

2. Fairness and Impartiality: God's righteousness is characterized by perfect fairness and impartiality. He treats all individuals equitably, without favoritism or bias. In the context of justice, this means that His judgments are not swayed by personal preferences or external influences.

3. Justice as a Reflection of God's Character: The justice of God is a reflection of His righteousness. His judgments are always in line with His moral perfection. Romans underscores that human justice should mirror this divine attribute. In other words, human justice should aim to be in accordance with God's righteous character.

4. Alignment with Divine Will: Justice, according to God's righteousness, means aligning human laws, actions, and decisions with God's will and moral standards. Romans teaches that when human justice aligns with God's righteousness, it contributes to the establishment of a just and equitable society.

5. Restoration and Reconciliation: God's righteousness also encompasses His desire for the restoration and reconciliation of

humanity. In the Christian tradition, this is exemplified through the sacrificial work of Jesus Christ, which offers redemption and reconciliation to those who have sinned.

Hence, God's righteousness, as emphasized in the Book of Romans, is the ultimate standard of moral and ethical perfection. It serves as the basis for understanding justice, with the expectation that human justice should strive to align with God's character, ensuring fairness, impartiality, and the pursuit of righteousness in all aspects of society.

In the Book of Romans, there is a significant exploration of the relationship between justice and the Mosaic Law. The Mosaic Law refers to the religious and legal code given to the Israelites through Moses, which includes the Ten Commandments and various other statutes and commandments. Here is how Romans addresses this relationship:

1. The Law Reveals God's Standard of Justice:

Romans 3:20 - "Therefore no one will be declared righteous in God's sight by the works of the law; rather, through the law, we become conscious of our sin."

This verse underscores the important role of the Mosaic Law in revealing God's standard of justice. It makes people conscious of their sin by providing a clear moral framework. The law serves as a divine guideline for righteousness and fairness, setting the standard for justice.

2. The Limitations of the Law in Justification:

Romans 3:28 - "For we maintain that a person is justified by faith apart from the works of the law."

This verse highlights a central theological point in Romans: that individuals are justified, or declared righteous, not through strict adherence to the Mosaic Law but through faith in Jesus Christ. The law, while revealing God's standard of justice, cannot, on its own, make individuals righteous in God's sight.

3. The Law Magnifies Sin:

Romans 7:7 - "What shall we say, then? Is the law sinful? Certainly not! Nevertheless, I would not have known what sin was had it not been for the law."

The law, as described in Romans, is not sinful. Instead, it magnifies sin by making individuals aware of their transgressions. It serves as a mirror that reflects human shortcomings and sinfulness, demonstrating the need for redemption and a just means of reconciliation.

4. Faith as the Path to Righteousness:

Romans 3:22 - "This righteousness is given through faith in Jesus Christ to all who believe."

Romans asserts that faith in Jesus Christ is the path to righteousness and justification. This faith aligns with God's ultimate standard of justice and offers the means of being declared righteous before God.

Romans emphasizes that the Mosaic Law plays a vital role in revealing God's standard of justice and moral righteousness. However, it also emphasizes that the law, on its own, cannot make individuals righteous. Instead, righteousness and justification come through faith in Jesus Christ, who embodies the ultimate fulfillment of God's justice and offers a means of reconciliation for humanity. This understanding is fundamental in Christian theology and informs discussions of justice, righteousness, and redemption.

Justification by Faith is a central theme in the Book of Romans and a foundational concept in Christian theology. It is pivotal to understanding justice as presented in Romans. Justification by faith means that individuals are declared righteous before God not by their own works or adherence to the law, but by placing their faith in Jesus Christ. This concept emphasizes the divine aspect of justice in the following ways:

1. Righteousness Through Faith:

Romans 3:22-24 - "This righteousness is given through faith in Jesus Christ to all who believe. There is no difference, for all have sinned and fall short of the glory of God, and all are justified freely by his grace through the redemption that came by Christ Jesus."

This passage underscores that righteousness is granted to individuals who believe in Jesus Christ. It highlights that all have sinned and fallen short of God's glory, but justification is freely provided through God's grace and redemption in Christ. This divine act of justification through faith is a cornerstone of the book's message.

2. Salvation Through Faith:

Romans 5:1 - "Therefore, since we have been justified through faith, we have peace with God through our Lord Jesus Christ."

Justification by faith leads to reconciliation with God, symbolizing the divine aspect of justice. This verse explains that faith brings peace with God, indicating that God's justice is not solely punitive but seeks reconciliation and restoration.

3. Divine Grace:

Romans 3:28 - "For we maintain that a person is justified by faith apart from the works of the law."

The book makes it clear that justification by faith is not achieved through human efforts or adherence to legalistic works. This concept emphasizes divine grace and the idea that God's justice is extended to humanity as a gift, demonstrating the divine attribute of compassion and fairness.

4. Inclusivity:

Romans 10:12 - "For there is no difference between Jew and Gentile—the same Lord is Lord of all and richly blesses all who call on him."

Justification by faith is inclusive, emphasizing that it is available to all, regardless of their background or heritage. This aligns with the divine justice that transcends human boundaries and offers salvation to everyone.

Therefore, justification by faith, as expounded in the Book of Romans, demonstrates the divine aspect of justice. It signifies that righteousness, reconciliation, and salvation come through faith in Jesus Christ, emphasizing that God's justice is marked by grace, inclusivity, and the desire to bring humanity into a restored relationship with Him.

The relationship between justice and mercy is a central theme in the Book of Romans. Romans' grapples with the balance between God's justice and His mercy, and it underscores how these two attributes are harmonized through the sacrifice of Christ. Here are Bible verses that exemplify this balance:

1. God's Justice and Mercy in Christ's Sacrifice:

Romans 3:23-24 - "For all have sinned and fall short of the glory of God, and all are justified freely by his grace through the redemption that came by Christ Jesus."

This verse highlights the universality of human sin and the need for redemption. God's justice is evident in the fact that all have sinned and fallen short of His glory. However, His mercy is equally evident in the free justification offered through the redemptive work of Christ. It demonstrates the harmonization of justice and mercy through Christ's sacrifice.

2. Justice Satisfied Through the Atonement:

Romans 3:25 - "God presented Christ as a sacrifice of atonement, through the shedding of his blood—to be received by faith. He did this to demonstrate his righteousness because in his forbearance he had left the sins committed beforehand unpunished."

This verse illustrates that God presented Christ as a sacrifice of atonement, satisfying His justice by shedding His blood. At the same time, it emphasizes God's forbearance, indicating His mercy in not immediately punishing sins committed beforehand. The sacrifice of Christ demonstrates both justice and mercy in God's plan of salvation.

3. Salvation by Grace Through Faith:

Romans 3:28 - "For we maintain that a person is justified by faith apart from the works of the law."

Romans makes it clear that salvation is not earned through human efforts or adherence to the law but is received by faith. This emphasizes God's mercy in freely granting justification to those who believe, showcasing His loving kindness and the balance between justice and mercy.

4. God's Mercy Toward All:

Romans 11:32 - "For God has bound everyone over to disobedience so that he may have mercy on them all."

This verse illustrates God's overarching plan, where all have fallen into disobedience, but He extends mercy to all. It shows that God's justice and mercy work in harmony, with His ultimate desire to extend mercy to humanity.

Accordingly, the Book of Romans demonstrates how God's justice, as depicted in the book, is harmonized with His mercy through the sacrifice of Christ. It reveals the balance between the recognition of human sin and the free gift of salvation through faith, highlighting God's attributes of justice and mercy working together in His redemptive plan.

"Justice for All" in the context of restorative justice is a principle that underscores the universality of the application of justice. It aligns with a commitment to fairness, inclusivity, and equity in the justice system and society as a whole. The concept of "Justice for All" and its alignment with a just and equitable society can be discussed with reference to the inclusivity emphasized in the Book of Romans:

1. Inclusivity in Salvation:

The Book of Romans stresses that the message of salvation is for all, regardless of their backgrounds or heritage. It explicitly states that there is no difference between Jew and Gentile, and that the Lord is the Lord of all (Romans 10:12). This inclusivity aligns with the idea of a just and equitable society where no one is excluded or discriminated against based on their origin or identity.

2. Universal Application of Justice:

In the context of restorative justice, the principle of "Justice for All" implies that the application of justice should be universal. Restorative justice seeks to provide a fair and equitable process for all individuals involved, including victims, offenders, and the community. It focuses on addressing harm and promoting healing without regard to factors such as race, religion, gender, or socio-economic status.

3. Addressing Systemic Injustices:

Restorative justice aims to address systemic injustices within the justice system. By acknowledging and rectifying these inequalities, it works towards a more just and equitable society. This aligns with the inclusivity emphasized in Romans, where salvation is extended to all, regardless of their previous state.

4. Community Involvement:

The Book of Romans also highlights the idea of a united community. In the context of restorative justice, involving the community in the resolution process fosters a sense of inclusivity and collective responsibility for justice. This communal involvement aligns with the idea of building a just and equitable society where individuals work together for the common good.

"Justice for All" in the context of restorative justice aligns with the principles of inclusivity and equity emphasized in the Book of Romans. It underscores the importance of ensuring that justice is accessible to all individuals, regardless of their backgrounds, and it promotes a vision of a just and equitable society where fairness and inclusivity are paramount.

Justice and Sin are fundamental concepts in the Bible, and they are addressed in the Book of Romans, shedding light on the consequences of sin and the need for redemption. Here's how Romans addresses these aspects:

1. Justice in the Face of Sin:

Romans highlights that God's justice requires accountability for sin. The book underscores that all have sinned and fallen short of the glory of God (Romans 3:23). This acknowledgment of human sinfulness forms the basis for God's justice, as it necessitates the recognition and addressing of wrongdoing.

2. Consequences of Sin: Romans delves into the consequences of sin, emphasizing that the wages of sin is death (Romans 6:23). This implies that sin leads to separation from God and spiritual death. Recognizing the gravity of sin and its consequences is integral to understanding the justice-seeking aspect of God's character. Justice, in this context, means holding individuals accountable for their actions.

3. The Need for Redemption:

Romans addresses the need for redemption from the consequences of sin. It teaches that God offers a solution to the problem of sin through the sacrifice of Christ. This redemption is not achieved through human efforts but is a gift of God's grace (Romans 3:24). The concept of redemption aligns with God's justice in that it provides a means to address the injustices caused by sin.

4. The Role of Faith:

Romans underscores that faith in Christ is the means of redemption and justification (Romans 5:1). This highlights that God's justice is not simply punitive but also restorative. It is about reconciling humanity with God and offering a path to righteousness through faith.

5. Harmony of Justice and Mercy:

By providing a means of redemption through Christ, Romans demonstrates the harmony of God's justice and mercy. It shows that God's justice is not solely about retribution but is also about reconciliation. In this sense, justice and mercy work together to offer a path to restoration.

Understanding the consequences of sin and the need for redemption is foundational to grasping the justice-seeking aspect of God's character as presented in the Book of Romans. It highlights the importance of recognizing the gravity of sin while emphasizing the opportunity for redemption and reconciliation through faith in Christ, thus aligning with the concept of God's justice in a biblical context.

The deep theological underpinnings of justice within the Christian tradition, as presented in the Book of Romans, can be summarized as follows:

1. God's Righteousness as the Standard: Romans emphasizes that God is the ultimate standard of moral and ethical

perfection. His righteousness serves as the foundation for justice. The justice in the Christian tradition aligns with God's character, and human justice should aim to mirror this divine standard.

2. Universal Sinfulness and the Need for Justice: The book underscores the universal human condition of sin. All have sinned and fallen short of God's glory (Romans 3:23). Recognizing the reality of sin is fundamental to understanding the justice-seeking aspect of God's character, which requires accountability for wrongdoing.

3. Justification by Faith: Romans introduces the concept of justification by faith, which means individuals are declared righteous before God through faith in Jesus Christ. This emphasizes that justice is not achieved through human efforts or adherence to the law but is a gift of God's grace.

4. Harmony of Justice and Mercy: Romans demonstrates the harmony of God's justice and mercy. While justice requires accountability for sin, it is balanced by God's mercy, which offers redemption and reconciliation. The sacrifice of Christ exemplifies this harmony, providing a means for both justice and mercy to coexist.

5. Inclusivity and Equity: Romans emphasizes inclusivity in the salvation message, stating that there is no difference between Jew and Gentile; the Lord is the Lord of all (Romans 10:12). This inclusivity aligns with the idea of a just and equitable society where justice is available to all, regardless of their backgrounds.

6. Redemption and Restoration: The book addresses the need for redemption and the restoration of the broken relationship between humanity and God. This theme of redemption

demonstrates that justice in the Christian tradition is not solely about punishment but also about restoration and reconciliation.

7. Faith as a Path to Righteousness: Romans teaches that faith in Christ is the means to righteousness and reconciliation. This concept emphasizes the divine aspect of justice, highlighting that righteousness and justification come through faith in Jesus Christ, aligning with God's character.

The theological underpinnings of justice in the Christian tradition, as presented in the Book of Romans, revolve around God's righteousness as the standard, the recognition of universal sinfulness, and the need for redemption through faith. It showcases the harmony of justice and mercy, inclusivity, and the overarching goal of reconciliation and restoration, all rooted in the character and teachings of God as revealed in the Bible.

Restorative justice principles can align with the teachings of the Book of Romans in several ways:

1. Reconciliation and Restoration: Restorative justice emphasizes the importance of reconciling the offender, victim, and the community. Romans also underscores the need for reconciliation, highlighting that through faith in Christ, individuals can be reconciled to God. Both restorative justice and Romans emphasize the importance of healing and restoration.

2. Accountability and Repentance: Restorative justice encourages offenders to take responsibility for their actions and make amends. Romans emphasizes repentance and turning away from sin as an essential aspect of redemption. This shared emphasis on accountability and transformation aligns with both approaches.

3. Inclusivity: Restorative justice seeks to involve all affected parties, ensuring inclusivity in the decision-making process. Romans emphasizes inclusivity in salvation, stating that there is no difference between Jew and Gentile. This principle aligns with the idea that justice should be accessible to all, regardless of their background.

4. Community Involvement: Restorative justice often involves the community in the resolution process. Romans highlights the significance of the Christian community in promoting reconciliation and healing. Both emphasize the role of the community in the process of justice and restoration.

5. Forgiveness and Mercy: Restorative justice encourages victims to consider forgiveness, which can lead to healing. Romans discusses the role of forgiveness and mercy in the context of salvation and redemption, reflecting the broader themes of forgiveness and healing in both approaches.

6. Balancing Justice and Grace: Restorative justice seeks to balance the need for accountability with a focus on healing and reconciliation. Romans addresses the balance between justice and mercy, emphasizing that God's justice is harmonized with His mercy through the sacrifice of Christ. This shared emphasis on balance reflects a holistic approach to justice.

7. Redemption and Transformation: Restorative justice emphasizes the potential for the transformation of offenders. Romans teaches that faith in Christ can lead to redemption and a new life. Both approaches highlight the possibility of personal growth and change.

The culmination of Paul's argument in Romans 1–3 reveals that his own liberation came not through the observance of the "works of the law" but through a revelation of Jesus Christ. This revelation marks the resolution to the problem of idolatry: "The justice of God is revealed through the faithfulness of Jesus Christ for all who believe" (3:22).

Throughout the first three chapters, the term "justice" is interwoven with concepts of injustice, God's decree, and just judgment—all derived from the root "dik." Another term, "justification," signifies how God will rectify and usher in healing and reconciliation.

Contrary to the perspective held by Saul the Pharisee, where "justice" led to the persecution of Jesus' followers, Paul the Apostle now asserts that justice entails reconciliation. This transformative disclosure occurs on an epoch-defining scale, with God's primary work being to "make known," enlighten minds, and dispel the darkness that had shrouded the awareness of idolaters.

The "law and prophets" bear witness to God's revelation of true justice (3:21-22). They have consistently conveyed this message. To be just means to love God and one's neighbor, blessing all the families of the earth. The law and prophets also attest to the pitfalls that emerge when the law becomes an idol that sustains injustice.

The faithfulness of Jesus, exemplified in his life, unveils God's justice. As Jesus emphasized, the law exists to serve humanity, not the other way around. Jesus' life of liberation from the dominion of the Powers and their idolatrous mechanisms "redeems" all who place their trust in his path as the authentic revelation of God's justice.

When Paul speaks of Jesus' blood as the means of "a sacrifice of atonement" presented by God, he references Jesus' self-sacrificial life, which culminated in his crucifixion—a testament to God's justice. God "presented Jesus" with the purpose of "manifesting God's justice" (3:25). Jesus' self-sacrifice was "effective" through his faithfulness (3:25). This comprehension of God's justice eradicates any basis for self-righteousness. Paul queries, "What becomes of boasting?" His response is unequivocal: "It is excluded" (3:27). All have equally engaged in idolatry, and all have equal access to the healing justice of God.

CHAPTER 03

PAUL'S PERSPECTIVE OF JUSTICE

The Apostle Paul's perspective on justice, as presented in the Book of Romans and his other writings, can be summarized as follows:

1. God's Righteousness: Paul emphasizes that God is the ultimate standard of righteousness and justice. His concept of justice is rooted in God's character, which is inherently just and fair. Paul's view aligns with the idea that human justice should mirror God's righteousness.

2. Universal Sinfulness: Paul acknowledges the universal human condition of sin, stating that "all have sinned and fall short of the glory of God" (Romans 3:23). This recognition of human sinfulness is a foundational aspect of justice in Paul's perspective.

3. Justification by Faith: Paul introduces the concept of justification by faith, which means that individuals are declared righteous before God not by their own works but through faith in Jesus Christ. This perspective emphasizes that justice is not

achieved through human efforts or adherence to the law but is a gift of God's grace.

4. Harmony of Justice and Mercy: Paul's writings demonstrate the harmonization of God's justice and mercy. While justice requires accountability for sin, it is balanced by God's mercy, which offers redemption and reconciliation. The sacrifice of Christ exemplifies this balance, providing a means for both justice and mercy to coexist.

5. Inclusivity: Paul emphasizes inclusivity in the salvation message, stating that there is no difference between Jew and Gentile; the Lord is the Lord of all (Romans 10:12). This inclusivity aligns with the idea of a just and equitable society where justice is available to all, regardless of their backgrounds.

6. Transformation and Renewal: Paul's perspective on justice goes beyond punishment and extends to the transformation and renewal of individuals. He encourages believers to be transformed by the renewing of their minds (Romans 12:2), reflecting the idea that justice involves personal growth and change.

7. Community and Reconciliation: Paul's writings emphasize the role of the Christian community in promoting reconciliation and restoration. This aligns with the restorative aspect of justice, where the community plays a crucial role in the healing process.

Therefore, Paul's perspective on justice is deeply rooted in God's righteousness, acknowledges human sinfulness, and emphasizes justification by faith as a means of achieving righteousness. It also highlights the harmony of justice and mercy, inclusivity, personal transformation, and the role of the Christian community in promoting reconciliation and restoration. This perspective has had a profound influence on Christian theology and understanding of justice.

Paul's understanding of God's justice, as presented in his writings including the Book of Romans, is deeply rooted in the following principles:

Paul perceives God's justice as intrinsically tied to His righteousness. God is the ultimate standard of moral and ethical perfection, and His justice is based on His character, which is inherently righteous and fair. This divine righteousness serves as the foundation for justice in the Christian tradition.

According to Paul, God's justice requires accountability. Human beings are held accountable for their actions, and God's justice demands that wrongdoing is addressed. Paul's understanding aligns with the idea that justice is about holding individuals responsible for their actions and upholding moral standards.

Paul views God's justice as a reflection of His character. In his perspective, God's judgments and actions are always in line with His righteous character. This perspective implies that human justice should aim to mirror God's character, ensuring fairness, impartiality, and alignment with divine moral standards.

While Paul underscores the importance of accountability and righteousness, he also emphasizes the role of God's grace in justice. He teaches that God's justice is harmonized with His mercy through the sacrifice of Christ. This perspective highlights the redemptive aspect of justice, where God offers a path to reconciliation and restoration.

Paul's understanding of God's justice has significant implications for human justice. It implies that human justice should align with God's righteousness and aim for fairness, impartiality, and moral standards. It also suggests that human justice should harmonize accountability with the possibility of redemption and reconciliation, reflecting the divine aspect of justice.

Paul perceives God's justice as based on divine righteousness, requiring accountability for human actions. His perspective emphasizes the balance between justice and mercy, with implications for how human justice should align with God's character and standards. This understanding of God's justice has had a profound influence on Christian theology and the concept of justice within the Christian tradition.

Paul's views on sin and accountability, as presented in his writings, especially in the Book of Romans, are deeply rooted in Christian theology. Here are some of his insights with Bible references:

1. The Universality of Sin:

Romans 3:23 - "For all have sinned and fall short of the glory of God."

Paul's teaching emphasizes the universal nature of sin. He states that all people have sinned and fallen short of God's glory, acknowledging the common human condition of sinfulness.

2. The Consequences of Sin:

Romans 6:23 - "For the wages of sin is death, but the gift of God is eternal life in Christ Jesus our Lord."

Paul teaches that sin leads to death, not only physical but also spiritual separation from God. The consequences of sin are significant, and he underscores the gravity of this reality.

3. Accountability Before God:

Romans 14:12 - "So then, each of us will give an account of ourselves to God."

Paul emphasizes individual accountability before God. He teaches that each person will give an account of their actions and decisions to God. This understanding is foundational to the concept of justice, as it necessitates responsibility for one's deeds.

4. The Role of the Law:

Romans 3:20 - "Therefore no one will be declared righteous in God's sight by the works of the law; rather, through the law we become conscious of our sin."

Paul discusses the role of the Mosaic Law in making individuals conscious of their sin. While the law reveals God's standard of justice, it cannot, on its own, make individuals righteous. It highlights the need for accountability and the limitations of human efforts in achieving righteousness.

5. The Need for Redemption:

Romans 3:24-25 - "and all are justified freely by his grace through the redemption that came by Christ Jesus. God presented Christ as a sacrifice of atonement, through the shedding of his blood."

Paul teaches that the need for accountability for sin is met through the redemption that comes through faith in Christ. God's justice is harmonized with His mercy through the sacrifice of Christ, providing a means of redemption and reconciliation.

In Paul's perspective, sin and accountability are central to the Christian understanding of justice. He emphasizes the universality of sin, the serious consequences of sin, and the need for individual accountability before God. His teachings also highlight the redemptive aspect of justice, where faith in Christ provides a way to address the consequences of sin and find reconciliation with God.

Paul's emphasis on redemption is a central theme in his writings, and it plays a significant role in understanding the justice-seeking aspect of God's character. Here are some Bible verses that underscore Paul's emphasis on redemption and its role in God's justice-seeking aspect:

1. Romans 3:24-25 - "and all are justified freely by his grace through the redemption that came by Christ Jesus. God presented Christ as a sacrifice of atonement, through the shedding of his blood."

In this passage, Paul highlights that redemption is made possible through the sacrifice of Christ. It is through this redemption that God's justice is satisfied, and reconciliation becomes attainable.

2. Romans 8:23-24 - "Not only so, but we ourselves, who have the first fruits of the Spirit, groan inwardly as we wait eagerly for our adoption to sonship, the redemption of our bodies. For in this hope, we were saved."

Paul emphasizes the future aspect of redemption, not only for the individual but also for creation itself. This redemption is part of the hope of salvation and the ultimate plan of God's justice.

3. Ephesians 1:7 - "In him we have redemption through his blood, the forgiveness of sins, in accordance with the riches of God's grace."

Paul's letter to the Ephesians underscores that redemption is achieved through the blood of Christ. This redemption includes forgiveness of sins and is a demonstration of God's grace.

4. Colossians 1:14 - "in whom we have redemption, the forgiveness of sins."

The Book of Colossians reiterates the concept of redemption as the means for the forgiveness of sins. It emphasizes that redemption is achieved through Christ.

5. Titus 2:14 - "who gave himself for us to redeem us from all wickedness and to purify for himself a people that are his very own, eager to do what is good."

Paul's letter to Titus emphasizes that Christ gave himself to redeem people from wickedness. This redemption leads to purification and the transformation of individuals, aligning with God's justice-seeking aspect.

Paul's emphasis on redemption is closely tied to God's justice-seeking aspect. Redemption through faith in Christ provides a means for addressing the consequences of sin, achieving reconciliation, and ultimately satisfying God's justice. It demonstrates the harmonization of justice and mercy, with redemption being a pivotal aspect of this theological perspective.

In Paul's theology, reconciliation and restoration are central themes that are discussed in both human relationships and the broader divine plan of salvation. Here are some key aspects of Paul's teachings on reconciliation and restoration, along with relevant Bible references:

Reconciliation in Human Relationships:

1. Reconciliation with God: In Paul's theology, reconciliation primarily refers to the restoration of the broken relationship between humanity and God. This reconciliation is made possible through faith in Christ.

- 2 Corinthians 5:18 "All this is from God, who reconciled us to himself through Christ and gave us the ministry of reconciliation."

2. Reconciliation with Others: Paul emphasizes the importance of reconciling with one another in the Christian community. Believers are encouraged to seek peace and unity in their relationships.

- Ephesians 4:32 - "Be kind and compassionate to one another, forgiving each other, just as in Christ God forgave you."

3. Restoration of Sinners: Paul teaches that when a fellow believer falls into sin, the goal is not condemnation but restoration. The community should seek to restore the person to a right relationship with God.

- Galatians 6:1 - "Brothers and sisters, if someone is caught in a sin, you who live by the Spirit should restore that person gently. But watch yourselves, or you also may be tempted."

Restoration in the Broader Divine Plan:

1. Restoration of Creation: Paul's theology includes the concept that the entire creation is in the process of restoration. The effects of sin on creation will be reversed, and it will be restored to its intended state.

- Romans 8:21 - "that the creation itself will be liberated from its bondage to decay and brought into the freedom and glory of the children of God."

2. Reconciliation of All Things: Paul teaches that through Christ, God is reconciling all things to Himself, whether things on earth or in heaven. This emphasizes the comprehensive nature of God's plan for restoration.

- Colossians 1:20 - "and through him to reconcile to himself all things, whether things on earth or things in heaven, by making peace through his blood, shed on the cross."

3. Restoration of Humanity: Central to Paul's theology is the restoration of humanity through faith in Christ. Those who believe are reconciled to God and experience personal transformation.

- 2 Corinthians 5:17 - "Therefore, if anyone is in Christ, the new creation has come: The old has gone, the new is here!"

Paul's teachings on reconciliation and restoration highlight the redemptive and transformative aspects of the Christian faith. They show that through faith in Christ, individuals can be reconciled with God, with one another, and even with the entire created order. This perspective aligns with the broader divine plan of salvation, where God seeks to restore all things to their intended state, demonstrating His justice and mercy.

Paul's writings, particularly in the Book of Romans and his other letters, provide a balanced perspective on the justice and mercy of God, with a significant emphasis on the role of grace in the redemption of humanity. Here's an analysis of Paul's perspective on mercy and grace:

1. Justice and Mercy Balance:

Paul's writings strike a balance between the justice and mercy of God. He acknowledges the justice of God in holding humanity accountable for sin and the consequences of sin, as discussed in Romans. However, Paul emphasizes that God's mercy is equally vital and is manifested through the redemptive work of Christ.

2. Role of Grace:

Paul places a strong emphasis on God's grace as the means by which humanity is redeemed. He teaches that salvation is not earned through human efforts but is a gift of God's grace. This grace is exemplified through the sacrifice of Christ on the cross.

3. Justification by Faith:

Paul's perspective on mercy and grace is closely tied to the concept of justification by faith. He teaches that individuals are declared righteous before God not by their own works but through faith in Jesus Christ. This emphasizes that God's mercy is extended to all who believe and that grace is the foundation of this divine action.

4. Redemptive Nature of Grace:

Paul views God's grace as redemptive in nature. It provides a means for individuals to be reconciled with God and experience transformation. Grace not only forgives sins but also empowers believers to live a new life in Christ.

5. Unmerited Favor:

Paul often describes God's grace as unmerited favor. It underscores the idea that grace is given freely and generously, despite human unworthiness. This perspective aligns with the concept of mercy, where God shows kindness and compassion even when it is not deserved.

6. Mercy and Grace in the Midst of Sin:

Paul's perspective on mercy and grace is particularly evident in his discussions about human sinfulness. He teaches that while all have sinned, God's mercy and grace are extended to offer forgiveness and redemption.

7. The Harmony of Justice and Mercy:

In Paul's writings, the harmony of justice and mercy is evident. God's justice is met through Christ's sacrifice, and His mercy is extended to those who place their faith in Him. This balance highlights the redemptive and restorative aspect of God's character.

Paul's perspective on mercy and grace demonstrates the harmonization of justice and mercy in the redemptive plan of God. He emphasizes that salvation is achieved through God's grace, which is freely given to all who believe. Grace is the foundation of redemption and restoration, showcasing the divine character that extends both justice and mercy to humanity.

The perspectives presented by Paul in the Book of Romans have several practical implications for justice, including restorative justice principles:

1. Redemptive Justice: Paul's emphasis on redemption through faith in Christ provides a basis for a redemptive approach

to justice. Restorative justice principles align with this perspective by emphasizing the potential for transformation and the opportunity for offenders to make amends.

2. Community Involvement: Paul's teachings on reconciliation and the role of the Christian community in promoting restoration have practical implications for restorative justice. Restorative justice often involves bringing together victims, offenders, and the community to participate in the resolution process, fostering community involvement and accountability.

3. Accountability and Healing: Paul's view of individual accountability and the need for repentance aligns with restorative justice principles. In restorative justice, accountability is a key component, but it is combined with a focus on healing and restoration, rather than mere punishment.

4. Inclusivity: Paul's teachings on the inclusivity of salvation, where there is no distinction between Jew and Gentile, emphasize that justice should be accessible to all. Restorative justice principles also stress inclusivity, ensuring that the process is available to all individuals, regardless of their backgrounds.

5. Balance of Justice and Mercy: Paul's perspective on the harmony of justice and mercy is applicable to restorative justice. This approach seeks to balance accountability for wrongdoing with a focus on reconciliation and healing, reflecting the redemptive and merciful aspects of justice.

6. Forgiveness and Reconciliation: Paul's teachings on forgiveness and reconciliation are fundamental to both Christian theology and restorative justice. Both perspectives encourage the

restoration of relationships and the healing of harm caused by wrongdoing.

7. Transformation: Paul's teachings on personal transformation align with restorative justice principles that aim to address the root causes of criminal behavior and promote the growth and change of offenders.

8. Principles of Fairness and Equity: Paul's emphasis on the righteousness of God as the standard of justice encourages a just and equitable approach to justice. Restorative justice principles aim to provide fairness and equity in the resolution process.

Incorporating Paul's perspectives into practical approaches to justice, including restorative justice principles, can lead to a more holistic and redemptive form of justice. It emphasizes accountability, reconciliation, inclusivity, and healing, while also reflecting the redemptive and merciful character of God, as revealed in the Book of Romans.

Certainly, exploring Paul's views on justice, reconciliation, and restoration in the context of the Book of Romans provides valuable insights into Christian theology and the practical implications of these concepts. Here's a summary of Paul's views:

1. Justice:

Paul's perspective on justice is rooted in the righteousness of God. He teaches that God is the ultimate standard of justice, and human justice should align with His character. Paul acknowledges the universality of sin and the need for accountability, emphasizing that all have sinned and fallen short of God's glory (Romans 3:23). This recognition of human sinfulness forms the basis for God's justice, which requires accountability for wrongdoing. Paul's writings also highlight the redemptive and transformative aspect of justice, where faith in Christ provides a means of reconciliation and restoration.

2. Reconciliation:

Paul emphasizes reconciliation in two significant ways. First, he underscores the reconciliation of individuals with God through faith in Christ. Through Christ's sacrifice, people can be reconciled to God, despite their sinful nature. Second, Paul encourages believers to seek reconciliation with one another in the Christian community. He promotes peace and unity among believers, emphasizing forgiveness and compassion as essential aspects of reconciliation.

3. Restoration:

Paul's views on restoration are closely linked to the redemptive aspect of justice. He teaches that individuals who have faith in Christ become new creations (2 Corinthians 5:17). This transformation reflects the restorative nature of God's justice, where broken relationships can be healed, and individuals can experience personal growth and change. Additionally, Paul's theology includes the broader concept of the restoration of creation itself. He envisions a future where the effects of sin on the entire created order will be reversed, and it will be restored to its intended state.

Overall, Paul's views on justice, reconciliation, and restoration in the Book of Romans highlight the redemptive and transformative aspects of the Christian faith. They emphasize that justice involves more than punishment; it involves accountability, reconciliation, healing, and restoration. These perspectives continue to shape Christian theology and have practical implications for approaches to justice, including restorative justice principles.

The theological foundations of justice within the Christian tradition, as influenced by the writings of figures like the Apostle Paul in the Book of Romans, have significant relevance to modern discussions of restorative justice. Here's a deeper understanding of these foundations and their contemporary significance:

1. Justice as Rooted in God's Righteousness:

The Christian tradition, as articulated by Paul in Romans, establishes justice as rooted in God's righteousness. This divine righteousness serves as the standard for justice. In modern discussions of restorative justice, this perspective highlights the importance of aligning human justice with moral and ethical principles grounded in God's character. It calls for justice systems that seek to reflect the divine standard of righteousness in their decisions and actions.

2. Universal Sinfulness and Accountability:

The Christian understanding of justice acknowledges the universal sinfulness of humanity, as all have sinned and fallen short of God's glory (Romans 3:23). In contemporary discussions, this recognition of universal sinfulness underlines the need for accountability in restorative justice. It acknowledges that all individuals, regardless of their background, may be capable of wrongdoing, and restorative justice principles provide a means to address and heal harm in a way that promotes accountability and transformation.

3. Redemptive and Restorative Justice:

Paul's emphasis on redemption and restoration through faith in Christ highlights the redemptive and restorative aspects of justice. In modern discussions of restorative justice, this concept underscores the importance of addressing the root causes of harm and promoting the transformation of offenders. It aligns with the idea that justice should aim not only for punishment but also for the healing and restoration of individuals and relationships.

4. Inclusivity and Equity:

Paul's teaching that there is no distinction between Jew and Gentile in salvation (Romans 10:12) emphasizes inclusivity. In discussions of modern restorative justice, this principle highlights the need for justice systems that are accessible to all individuals, regardless of their backgrounds. It promotes a more equitable and just approach to resolving conflicts and addressing harm.

5. Balance of Justice and Mercy:

The harmonization of justice and mercy in Paul's theology reflects the contemporary pursuit of balancing accountability with the restoration of individuals and communities. It encourages a more holistic approach to justice that recognizes the need for accountability while also offering pathways to reconciliation and healing.

The theological foundations of justice within the Christian tradition, as presented in the Book of Romans and influenced by the writings of the Apostle Paul, continue to provide a profound and relevant framework for modern discussions of restorative justice. They highlight the importance of aligning justice with divine standards, recognizing the universal nature of sin, promoting redemption and restoration, ensuring inclusivity, and balancing accountability with mercy. These principles have enduring relevance and can inform contemporary efforts to create more just and restorative approaches to addressing harm and conflict.

46

CHAPTER 04

SIN AND ITS CONSEQUENCES

Sin is a central theme in Paul's writings, and understanding its nature and consequences is essential to comprehending the redemptive and restorative aspects of justice.

In the context of the Book of Romans, sin is a central theme, and its consequences are thoroughly explored. Here's a summary of how sin and its consequences are construed in Romans:

1. Universality of Sin:

Paul makes it clear that all human beings have sinned and fallen short of the glory of God (Romans 3:23). This universal recognition of sinfulness sets the stage for understanding the consequences of sin.

2. Consequences of Sin:

The consequences of sin are profound and include separation from God. Paul teaches that the wages of sin is death (Romans 6:23), signifying both physical and spiritual separation from God. This separation is a significant consequence of sin.

3. Accountability:

In Romans, Paul emphasizes individual accountability for sin. He teaches that each person will give an account of their actions to God (Romans 14:12). This accountability is a key aspect of understanding the consequences of sin.

4. Root of Harm:

Sin is often at the root of harm in human relationships and societies. It leads to conflict, brokenness, and injustice. This understanding of sin as the source of harm underscores the relevance of restorative justice, which seeks to address and repair the harm caused by wrongdoing.

5. Restoration as a Response:

Romans also presents the concept of restoration and redemption. Paul emphasizes that the consequences of sin can be addressed through faith in Christ. This aligns with the restorative aspect of justice, which aims to repair harm, promote reconciliation, and facilitate the restoration of individuals and relationships.

6. Practical Implications:

Understanding sin and its consequences in the context of Romans has practical implications for restorative justice. It highlights the need for accountability while also emphasizing the redemptive and restorative potential of justice. In resolving conflicts and addressing the harm caused by sin, restorative justice principles can provide a framework that seeks both accountability and healing.

The Book of Romans presents sin as a universal reality with profound consequences, including separation from God and the need for accountability. Understanding these consequences provides the foundation for addressing harm and promoting restoration, which aligns with the principles of restorative justice in modern discussions of justice and reconciliation.

The concept of sin in the Book of Romans and its implications for restorative justice can be summarized as follows:

1. The Universality of Sin:

In the Book of Romans, the Apostle Paul emphasizes the universal nature of sin. He states that "all have sinned and fall short of the glory of God" (Romans 3:23). This recognition of universal human sinfulness forms the basis for understanding the need for justice and accountability in addressing wrongdoing.

2. The Consequences of Sin:

Paul teaches that the consequences of sin are profound. He asserts that "the wages of sin is death" (Romans 6:23), signifying not only physical death but also spiritual separation from God. This understanding of the consequences of sin highlights the need for addressing the harm and brokenness caused by wrongdoing.

3. Root of Harm in Human Relationships:

Sin is often at the root of harm in human relationships and societies. It leads to conflicts, brokenness, and injustices. Restorative justice principles acknowledge that sin is a source of harm and aim to repair the damage caused by wrongdoing, promoting reconciliation and healing.

4. Restorative Response to Sin:

Paul's theology in Romans emphasizes the redemptive and restorative aspect of justice. He teaches that individuals can be justified and reconciled to God through faith in Christ. This aligns with the principles of restorative justice, which seek to repair harm, promote reconciliation, and restore individuals and relationships.

5. Accountability and Healing:

The concept of sin in Romans underscores the importance of individual accountability for wrongdoing. Restorative justice incorporates this accountability while also focusing on the healing and transformation of offenders. It aims to hold individuals responsible for their actions while providing them with an opportunity to make amends and reintegrate into the community.

6. Practical Implications:

Understanding the concept of sin in the Book of Romans has practical implications for restorative justice. It emphasizes the need for accountability while also highlighting the redemptive and restorative potential of justice. Restorative justice principles provide a framework for addressing harm caused by sin, seeking both accountability and healing in the process.

The concept of sin in the Book of Romans underscores the universality of sin, its consequences, and the need for accountability. It aligns with the principles of restorative justice, which seek to address harm, promote reconciliation, and restore individuals and relationships in response to sin and wrongdoing.

The universality of sin, as taught by the Apostle Paul in the Book of Romans, is the concept that all human beings, regardless of their background or circumstances, have sinned and fallen short of God's glory. This teaching emphasizes the following key points:

1. No Exception: According to Paul, there are no exceptions to the universality of sin. Every individual, without distinction, has

committed acts of wrongdoing or fallen short of God's perfect moral standard.

2. Recognition of Human Imperfection: This teaching acknowledges the fundamental imperfection and moral shortcomings of humanity. It recognizes that humans, in their fallen state, are incapable of attaining the divine standard of righteousness on their own.

3. Spiritual Implication: The recognition of universal sinfulness has significant spiritual implications. It underscores the separation between humanity and God due to sin. The consequences of sin include spiritual separation, which is described as "death" in Romans 6:23, indicating the loss of a relationship with the divine.

4. Basis for Accountability: The understanding of the universality of sin serves as the basis for individual accountability. It forms the foundation for the concept that all individuals are answerable for their actions and are in need of redemption and reconciliation with God.

5. Equality Before God: Paul's teaching on the universality of sin also underscores the equality of all individuals before God. It doesn't matter one's background, social status, or heritage; all are equally in need of God's grace and redemption.

6. Theological Significance: The universality of sin is a fundamental theological concept in Christian doctrine. It sets the stage for the need for salvation through faith in Christ and the redemptive aspect of Christian theology.

In summary, Paul's teaching on the universality of sin emphasizes that every individual, without exception, has sinned and fallen short of God's glory. This concept underlines the need for accountability, the recognition of human imperfection, and the universal need for redemption and reconciliation with God. It plays a central role in the theological framework of Christian doctrine, and it is relevant to discussions of justice and restorative justice, as it acknowledges the common human condition of sinfulness that justice systems seek to address.

The consequences of sin, as presented in the Bible, include both spiritual separation and the need for accountability. Here are some Bible verses that highlight these consequences:

1. Spiritual Separation:

- Isaiah 59:2 - "But your iniquities have separated you from your God; your sins have hidden his face from you, so that he will not hear."

This verse emphasizes that sin leads to spiritual separation from God. Iniquities and sins create a barrier that hinders a close relationship with the divine.

- Ephesians 2:1 - "As for you, you were dead in your transgressions and sins."

This verse underscores the spiritual consequences of sin, describing a state of spiritual death resulting from transgressions and sins.

2. The Need for Accountability:

- Romans 14:12 - "So then, each of us will give an account of ourselves to God."

This verse emphasizes individual accountability before God. It highlights the need for every person to give an account of their actions and choices.

- Galatians 6:7 - "Do not be deceived: God cannot be mocked. A man reaps what he sows."

This verse underlines the principle of accountability, indicating that individuals will experience the consequences of their actions. It relates the concept of sowing and reaping to personal responsibility.

- Romans 2:6 - "God 'will repay each person according to what they have done.'"

This verse reinforces the idea that God's justice includes accountability. Each person will be rewarded or repaid according to their deeds.

These verses illustrate the consequences of sin, emphasizing the spiritual separation it causes between individuals and God. They also stress the need for accountability, with individuals being responsible for their actions and facing the outcomes of their choices. These consequences are foundational to the understanding of justice and redemption, as they create the need for a redemptive and restorative response to address the harm and separation caused by sin.

The concept of "sin as the root of harm" signifies that wrongdoing, or sin, is often the underlying cause of harm, conflict, and brokenness in human relationships and societies. This understanding is rooted in biblical teachings and has implications for the relevance of restorative justice in addressing the consequences of sin. Here's a biblical exploration of this concept:

1. Genesis 3:16-19 - The Fall of Man:

In the story of Adam and Eve's disobedience in the Garden of Eden, sin is at the root of harm. Their sin led to a rupture in their relationship with God, with each other, and with the created order. Eve's desire for the forbidden fruit and Adam's participation in the sin resulted in consequences, including pain in childbirth, conflict in their relationship, and the toil of labor. This narrative illustrates how sin disrupts harmony and causes harm in various aspects of human life.

2. Genesis 4:1-16 - Cain and Abel:

The story of Cain and Abel exemplifies how sin leads to harm in human relationships. Cain's jealousy and anger over God's favoritism toward Abel ultimately led to the harm of his brother through murder. This narrative illustrates how unchecked sin can result in interpersonal harm and conflict.

3. Micah 2:1-2 - Covetousness and Injustice:

The prophet Micah speaks of covetousness and injustice in society, highlighting how the desire for more and the mistreatment of others can lead to harm. These actions are driven by sinful attitudes and have detrimental consequences for the vulnerable and marginalized.

4. Romans 3:10-18 - The Depravity of Humanity:

In Romans, Paul paints a comprehensive picture of the consequences of sin. He emphasizes the depravity of humanity, stating that "their throats are open graves; their tongues practice deceit; the poison of vipers is on their lips." This depravity results in harm, deception, and brokenness in human interactions.

5. Restorative Justice Relevance:

The concept of sin as the root of harm underscores the relevance of restorative justice. Restorative justice seeks to address the harm caused by wrongdoing and promotes accountability, healing, and reconciliation. It acknowledges that sin is often the cause of harm in human relationships and societies and provides a framework for repairing that harm. By focusing on restoration and reconciliation, restorative justice offers a redemptive response to the consequences of sin.

The biblical perspective of "sin as the root of harm" highlights that wrongdoing often leads to harm, conflict, and brokenness in human relationships and societies. This understanding underscores the relevance of restorative justice in addressing the consequences of sin by providing a framework for repairing harm, promoting accountability, and fostering healing and reconciliation in the face of harm caused by sin.

Restoration as a response to sin refers to a restorative approach to justice that aims to repair the harm caused by wrongdoing and reconcile individuals who have been affected. It emphasizes the redemptive and transformative aspect of justice. Here's an exploration of this concept:

1. Healing and Reconciliation:

A restorative response to sin focuses on healing the harm inflicted upon victims and seeks to reconcile offenders with those they have harmed. It recognizes that justice goes beyond punishment and aims to restore damaged relationships.

2. Accountability and Responsibility:

While restorative justice seeks healing and reconciliation, it also emphasizes accountability. Offenders are held responsible for their actions and are encouraged to take ownership of their wrongdoing. This accountability is an essential part of the restoration process.

3. Community Involvement:

Restorative justice often involves the community in the resolution process. Community members, including victims, offenders, and support networks, play a role in the restoration and reconciliation efforts. This community involvement can enhance the effectiveness of the process.

4. Transformation and Growth:

Restoration aims to facilitate the transformation and personal growth of offenders. It recognizes that individuals have the capacity to change and seeks to address the root causes of their behavior. This aspect aligns with the redemptive nature of justice, providing opportunities for individuals to make amends and reintegrate into society.

5. Healing of Wounds:

Restoration seeks to heal the wounds caused by sin. It acknowledges that harm has been done, but it also provides a pathway for healing and recovery, both for victims and offenders.

6. Justice and Mercy in Balance:

A restorative response to sin strikes a balance between justice and mercy. It acknowledges the need for accountability and the consequences of wrongdoing but also extends an offer of reconciliation and an opportunity for restoration.

7. Biblical Relevance:

Restorative justice principles align with the biblical concept of redemption and reconciliation. The teachings of forgiveness, reconciliation, and the restoration of relationships are central to Christian theology, emphasizing the redemptive aspect of justice.

Therefore, restoration as a response to sin in the context of restorative justice seeks to repair the harm caused by wrongdoing and reconcile individuals who have been affected. It combines accountability with healing, growth, and community involvement to promote reconciliation and transformation. This approach aligns with the redemptive and transformative aspect of justice found in both biblical teachings and contemporary discussions of justice.

Practical applications for addressing sin include recognizing its consequences and the need for accountability and healing. These principles inform restorative justice practices in contemporary discussions of addressing sin and conflict. Here's how:

1. Acknowledging the Consequences of Sin:

In the Book of Romans, the consequences of sin are made clear, emphasizing that sin leads to separation from God and spiritual death. Understanding these consequences informs restorative justice by recognizing the depth of harm caused by sin. Restorative justice acknowledges that wrongdoing harms individuals, communities, and relationships, and it seeks to address these harms.

2. Promoting Accountability:

Romans underscores the need for accountability, as each person will give an account of their actions to God (Romans 14:12). In restorative justice, accountability is a foundational principle. Offenders are encouraged to take responsibility for their actions, acknowledge the harm caused, and work toward making amends. This accountability helps restore a sense of justice and fairness in the aftermath of wrongdoing.

3. Focusing on Healing and Reconciliation:

The practical application of addressing sin, as informed by Romans, involves focusing on healing and reconciliation. Romans presents a redemptive and restorative response to sin through faith in Christ. Similarly, restorative justice aims to heal the harm caused by wrongdoing and promote reconciliation between offenders and victims. This process recognizes the importance of rebuilding relationships and fostering a sense of community.

4. Community Involvement:

Romans encourages a sense of community and mutual support among believers. In restorative justice practices, community involvement is vital. The community, including victims, offenders, and support networks, often plays a role in the resolution process. This community engagement contributes to the effectiveness of the restorative justice approach.

5. Balancing Justice and Mercy:

Romans harmonizes justice and mercy, and this balance is mirrored in restorative justice principles. While there is a focus on accountability and making amends, there is also room for mercy and grace. Restorative justice recognizes the potential for growth and transformation in individuals, promoting both justice and mercy.

The practical applications of addressing sin, as influenced by the Book of Romans, align with restorative justice principles.

These applications involve acknowledging the consequences of sin, promoting accountability, focusing on healing and reconciliation, involving the community, and striking a balance between justice and mercy. Restorative justice offers a framework for addressing sin and resolving conflicts that aligns with the redemptive and restorative aspects of justice found in the Book of Romans.

Practical applications for addressing sin, particularly in the context of restorative justice, involve several key principles:

1. Recognition of Consequences:

Practical applications begin with recognizing the consequences of sin. Understanding that wrongdoing can harm individuals, relationships, and communities is the first step. Restorative justice acknowledges these consequences and seeks to address them.

2. Accountability:

Sin carries a sense of individual responsibility. Practical applications include holding individuals accountable for their actions. In restorative justice, offenders are encouraged to take responsibility for their wrongdoing and make amends for the harm they've caused. This accountability is central to the process.

3. Healing and Restoration:

Addressing sin practically involves focusing on healing and restoration. Recognizing the need for healing the harm inflicted by sin, both on victims and offenders, is a key principle of restorative justice. This approach aims to repair the damage, restore relationships, and promote personal growth and transformation.

4. Community Involvement:

Practical applications in addressing sin often include community involvement. Restorative justice frequently includes victims, offenders, and support networks in the resolution process. The community plays a role in facilitating accountability, healing, and reconciliation.

5. Balancing Justice and Mercy:

Practical applications must balance justice and mercy. While accountability is important, there's also room for mercy and grace. Restorative justice acknowledges the potential for growth and change in individuals, promoting a holistic approach that considers both justice and mercy.

In essence, practical applications for addressing sin, guided by an understanding of its consequences, inform restorative justice practices. This approach recognizes the harm caused by wrongdoing, promotes accountability, emphasizes healing and restoration, involves the community, and balances justice with mercy. It provides a framework for addressing sin and resolving conflicts in a way that aligns with the redemptive and restorative aspects of justice found in various biblical teachings, including the Book of Romans.

CHAPTER 05

REDEMPTION AND ATONEMENT

Redemption and atonement as presented in the Book of Romans and their relevance to restorative justice. These themes are central to Christian theology and have significant implications for the practice of restorative justice.

1. Redemption:

Redemption refers to the act of saving or delivering someone from a state of bondage, captivity, or sin through the payment of a price or the offering of a sacrifice. In Christian theology, redemption is often associated with the work of Jesus Christ, who is seen as the Redeemer. The concept of redemption in the Book of Romans emphasizes that through faith in Christ, individuals can be saved from the consequences of sin and reconciled with God. This redemption is made possible by the sacrificial death of Christ, which is seen as the payment for humanity's sins.

2. Atonement:

Atonement involves the reconciliation of a relationship that has been broken or damaged. In Christianity, it often refers to the reconciliation between humanity and God. The process of atonement seeks to make amends for sin or wrongdoing and restore a harmonious relationship. In the Book of Romans, atonement is closely tied to the concept of justification by faith, which means that through faith in Christ, individuals can be declared righteous and reconciled with God. Christ's sacrifice is seen as the means of atonement, reconciling humanity with God by covering or removing the guilt of sin.

Redemption in Christian theology, as presented in the Book of Romans, is the act of saving individuals from the consequences of sin through the sacrifice of Christ. Atonement is the process of reconciling humanity with God, making amends for sin, and restoring a harmonious relationship through faith in Christ's redemptive work. These concepts are integral to the themes of salvation and reconciliation found in the Book of Romans and have relevance to discussions of justice and restorative justice.

In the Book of Romans, the concepts of redemption and atonement are closely tied to Christian theology and have relevance to the principles of restorative justice. Here's how these concepts are presented in Romans and their relevance to restorative justice:

In Romans, redemption is primarily associated with the work of Jesus Christ. Paul emphasizes that all have sinned and fallen short of God's glory (Romans 3:23) but can be justified freely by God's grace through the redemption that is in Christ Jesus (Romans 3:24). This redemption is made possible through Christ's sacrificial death, which is seen as the payment for humanity's sins. It signifies the act of saving individuals from the bondage of sin and reconciling them with God.

Restorative justice, like redemption, seeks to address the harm caused by wrongdoing and promote reconciliation. Redemption's relevance lies in its transformative power to heal and restore relationships. Restorative justice principles can align with the redemptive aspect of salvation by offering a framework for repairing harm, promoting reconciliation, and facilitating the restoration of individuals and relationships.

Atonement in Romans is closely tied to justification by faith. Paul teaches that through faith in Christ, individuals can be justified and reconciled with God. Christ's sacrificial death is seen as the means of atonement, reconciling humanity with God by covering or removing the guilt of sin. Romans emphasizes that through Christ, there is no condemnation for those who believe (Romans 8:1).

Atonement's relevance to restorative justice lies in the process of reconciliation. Restorative justice principles align with the concept of atonement by seeking to restore damaged relationships and promote reconciliation between offenders and victims. Just as Christ's atonement seeks to reconcile humanity with God, restorative justice seeks to reconcile individuals with those they've harmed, fostering healing and restoration.

The Book of Romans presents redemption and atonement as central themes in Christian theology, highlighting the transformative power of Christ's sacrifice. These concepts are relevant to restorative justice as they emphasize reconciliation, healing, and the restoration of individuals and relationships. Restorative justice principles align with the redemptive and atonement aspects of salvation by offering a framework for addressing harm and promoting reconciliation and restoration in response to wrongdoing.

Redemption and atonement themes are central to Christian theology and have significant implications for the practice of restorative justice for several reasons:

Theological Foundation:

Redemption and atonement are foundational to Christian theology because they address the central issue of sin and its consequences. According to Christian doctrine, all have sinned and fallen short of God's glory, and redemption and atonement through the work of Christ provide a solution to this problem.

Redemption and atonement in Christian theology are about reconciling humanity with God. This reconciliation involves making amends for wrongdoing, seeking forgiveness, and restoring a harmonious relationship. Similarly, restorative justice aims to reconcile individuals with those they have harmed, fostering healing and restoration.

Both redemption and atonement emphasize the transformative power of grace and forgiveness. In Christian theology, Christ's sacrifice is seen as a means of transformation and healing. Restorative justice principles similarly seek to transform offenders, promote accountability, and facilitate the healing of those affected by harm.

Redemption and atonement involve individuals taking responsibility for their actions and being held accountable. In the same way, restorative justice emphasizes accountability, where offenders take responsibility for their actions, acknowledge the harm they've caused, and work to make amends.

Both redemption and atonement involve the community or faith community. In Christian practice, the community plays a role in supporting individuals on their journey of redemption and atonement. In restorative justice, community involvement is central to the resolution process, as community members, including victims, offenders, and support networks, can facilitate reconciliation.

Redemption and atonement strike a balance between justice and mercy. They acknowledge the need for justice and accountability while extending an offer of mercy and forgiveness. Restorative justice principles similarly aim to balance these aspects by promoting justice through accountability while also offering opportunities for healing and reconciliation.

In summary, the themes of redemption and atonement in Christian theology have significant implications for restorative justice because they provide a theological foundation for addressing harm, seeking reconciliation, promoting transformation, and balancing justice with mercy. These themes are relevant to the practice of restorative justice as they emphasize the principles of accountability, healing, and the restoration of individuals and relationships.

The biblical understanding of redemption and atonement, especially as portrayed in the Book of Romans, emphasizes the role of Christ's sacrifice in the redemption of humanity. Let's explore these concepts with relevant Bible references:

Redemption in Romans:

In Romans, the concept of redemption is deeply rooted in the sacrifice of Jesus Christ as the means of salvation. The following verses highlight the biblical understanding of redemption:

- Romans 3:24-25 - "And all are justified freely by his grace through the redemption that came by Christ Jesus. God presented Christ as a sacrifice of atonement, through the shedding of his blood—to be received by faith."

These verses emphasize that redemption comes through Christ Jesus and is linked to His sacrifice. It is by God's grace that individuals are justified, and this justification is closely tied to redemption through the shedding of Christ's blood.

- Romans 5:8-9 - "But God demonstrates his own love for us in this: While we were still sinners, Christ died for us. Since we have now been justified by his blood, how much more shall we be saved from God's wrath through him!"

Here, the sacrificial death of Christ is presented as the means by which humanity is justified and saved from God's wrath, illustrating the redemptive nature of Christ's sacrifice.

The concept of atonement in Romans is closely related to justification by faith, where faith in Christ leads to reconciliation with God. These verses emphasize the role of Christ's sacrifice in atonement:

- Romans 5:10 - "For if, while we were God's enemies, we were reconciled to him through the death of his Son, how much more, having been reconciled, shall we be saved through his life!"

This verse highlights that reconciliation with God comes through the death of Christ, illustrating the concept of atonement. Christ's sacrifice paves the way for reconciliation and salvation.

- Romans 5:11 - "Not only is this so, but we also boast in God through our Lord Jesus Christ, through whom we have now received reconciliation."

Atonement is evident in the reconciliation received through Jesus Christ, signifying the restoration of a harmonious relationship with God.

Therefore, the Book of Romans provides a strong biblical understanding of redemption and atonement. These concepts are intimately connected to the sacrifice of Christ, emphasizing that through His sacrificial death, individuals can be justified, redeemed, and reconciled with God. This understanding is foundational to Christian theology and holds significant relevance for discussions of justice and restorative justice, as it underscores the transformative power of Christ's sacrifice in addressing the consequences of sin.

Restorative justice can be seen as a framework for achieving atonement in human relationships and communities, aligning with biblical principles. Let's explore this concept with relevant Bible verses:

1. Restorative Justice as Atonement:

Restorative justice, at its core, is concerned with repairing harm, fostering reconciliation, and promoting healing. These principles align with the concept of atonement in the following ways:

- Matthew 5:23-24 - "Therefore, if you are offering your gift at the altar and there remember that your brother or sister has something against you, leave your gift there in front of the altar. First, go and be reconciled to them; then come and offer your gift."

This verse emphasizes the importance of reconciliation before offering gifts or sacrifices to God. Restorative justice, like atonement, prioritizes reconciliation and addressing harm in relationships.

- Colossians 1:20 - "and through him to reconcile to himself all things, whether things on earth or things in heaven, by making peace through his blood, shed on the cross."

This verse highlights the role of Christ's sacrifice in reconciling all things. Restorative justice seeks to make peace and reconcile individuals by addressing harm, much like Christ's work on the cross.

2. Accountability and Responsibility:

Restorative justice emphasizes accountability and the responsibility of offenders. These principles align with the concept of atonement as individuals take responsibility for their actions and seek to make amends:

- 2 Corinthians 5:10 - "For we must all appear before the judgment seat of Christ, so that each of us may receive what is due us for the things done while in the body, whether good or bad."

Atonement and restorative justice both involve accountability, as individuals are called to give an account of their actions.

3. Community Involvement:

Restorative justice often involves the community or support networks in the resolution process. Community support aligns with the biblical principle of fellowship and mutual support:

- Romans 12:5 - "so in Christ we, though many, form one body, and each member belongs to all the others."

Community involvement is central to restorative justice, as community members, including victims, offenders, and support networks, participate in the process.

4. Balance of Justice and Mercy:

Atonement, as presented in the Bible, balances justice and mercy. Similarly, restorative justice seeks to balance justice with mercy, providing an opportunity for healing, redemption, and reconciliation:

- James 2:13 - "because judgment without mercy will be shown to anyone who has not been merciful. Mercy triumphs over judgment."

This verse emphasizes the triumph of mercy over judgment, aligning with the restorative justice principle of offering opportunities for personal growth and transformation.

Restorative justice can be viewed as a practical framework for achieving atonement in human relationships and communities. It aligns with the biblical principles of reconciliation, accountability, community involvement, and the balance of justice and mercy, making it a relevant approach to addressing harm and fostering atonement in the context of justice and reconciliation.

The transformative power of redemption is a central concept in both Christian theology and restorative justice. Here's how redemption leads to healing, reconciliation, and the restoration of individuals and relationships:

Christian Theology:

In Christian theology, redemption is the act of being saved from sin and its consequences through faith in Christ. The transformative power of redemption is evident in the following ways:

- Healing from Sin: Redemption involves healing individuals from the effects of sin. It offers forgiveness and freedom from guilt and condemnation. This healing allows individuals to experience inner peace and restoration.

- Reconciliation with God: Redemption reconciles individuals with God. Through the sacrifice of Christ, people are brought into a harmonious relationship with the divine. This reconciliation leads to a sense of wholeness and belonging.

- Transformation and Sanctification: Redemption goes beyond forgiveness; it initiates a process of personal transformation and sanctification. Believers are empowered to lead lives of righteousness and reflect Christ's character.

- Restoration of Brokenness: The transformative power of redemption is evident in the restoration of broken individuals and relationships. It offers hope and a fresh start to those who have experienced spiritual, emotional, or relational brokenness.

Restorative Justice:

Restorative justice shares the transformative aspects of redemption. It seeks to repair harm, foster reconciliation, and promote healing in the context of harm caused by wrongdoing. Here's how the transformative power of redemption is reflected in restorative justice:

-Healing of Harm: Restorative justice aims to heal the harm caused by wrongdoing, whether to individuals, communities, or relationships. It provides a space for victims to express their pain and for offenders to understand the impact of their actions.

- Reconciliation: Like redemption, restorative justice focuses on reconciliation. It offers a process through which individuals can reconcile, address the harm, and work toward mutual understanding.

- Empowering Accountability: Restorative justice holds offenders accountable for their actions, but it does so in a way that empowers personal growth and transformation. Offenders are encouraged to take responsibility for their wrongdoing and make amends.

- Community and Support: The community often plays a role in restorative justice processes, providing support for both victims and offenders. This community involvement aids in the transformation of individuals and relationships.

- Balancing Justice and Mercy: Restorative justice strikes a balance between justice and mercy, much like redemption. It seeks to deliver a just response to harm while offering opportunities for healing and restoration.

In both Christian theology and restorative justice, the transformative power of redemption is evident in the healing of harm, reconciliation, personal transformation, and the restoration of individuals and relationships. These concepts emphasize the redemptive and restorative aspects of justice, offering a path toward healing, reconciliation, and the transformation of individuals and communities.

Accountability and responsibility are integral to both the biblical understanding of atonement and the principles of restorative justice. These principles play a vital role in the atonement process. Here's how they contribute to atonement:

1. Biblical Understanding of Atonement:

In the Bible, atonement is closely linked to the idea of reconciling with God. This reconciliation often involves acknowledging one's wrongdoing, taking responsibility for it, and seeking forgiveness through a sacrificial offering. The importance of accountability and responsibility can be seen in the following ways:

- Acknowledging Sin: Atonement begins with acknowledging one's sin. This acknowledgment is an act of taking responsibility for one's actions. In the Old Testament, for example, individuals brought offerings to the altar as a symbol of acknowledging their sins.

- Repentance and Turning from Sin: Atonement often involves repentance, which includes not only feeling remorse for one's sins but also turning away from them. This act of turning away from sin demonstrates personal responsibility for one's actions.

- Offering Sacrifices: Sacrificial offerings were a common way to seek atonement in the Bible. The act of offering a sacrifice required individuals to take responsibility for their sins and actively seek reconciliation with God.

- Seeking Forgiveness: Atonement ultimately aims at seeking forgiveness from God. This requires individuals to take responsibility for their actions and express a desire to be reconciled with God through forgiveness.

2. Restorative Justice:

In restorative justice, accountability and responsibility are core principles. They are integral to the atonement process in the following ways:

- Acknowledging Harm: Atonement, within the context of restorative justice, involves acknowledging the harm caused to victims, the community, and relationships. Offenders are encouraged to take responsibility for the harm they've caused.

- Accepting Consequences: Restorative justice requires individuals to accept the consequences of their actions. This acknowledgment of responsibility is vital in the atonement process, as it shows a willingness to make amends.

- Making Amends: Taking responsibility includes making amends for one's actions. Offenders are expected to actively work towards repairing the harm they've caused, which aligns with the principle of accountability.

- Empowering Change: Restorative justice aims to empower individuals to change their behavior and make better choices in the future. This transformation is achieved through taking responsibility for one's actions and actively seeking personal growth.

Accountability and responsibility are important in the atonement process, both biblically and within the framework of restorative justice. They involve acknowledging wrongdoing, taking responsibility for one's actions, seeking forgiveness and making amends. These principles are integral to achieving reconciliation, healing, and restoration, whether in the context of one's relationship with God or in resolving conflicts in human relationships and communities.

The role of the community in the process of atonement is significant, as community involvement can support and enhance the atonement and redemption of individuals who have caused harm in various ways. Here's a discussion of the importance of community in the atonement process:

1. Support and Accountability:

Community involvement provides a support network for individuals seeking atonement and redemption. This support can be crucial in helping those who have caused harm to stay on the path of transformation. The community can offer encouragement, guidance, and accountability, which are essential for individuals to take responsibility for their actions and make amends.

2. Facilitating Reconciliation:

Atonement often involves reconciliation, both with the divine and with those who have been harmed. The community can play a facilitating role in bringing together offenders and victims, creating a safe space for dialogue and the restoration of relationships. Community support can help bridge the gap between parties involved, fostering understanding and forgiveness.

3. Community Service and Restitution:

Atonement may require individuals to engage in community service or make restitution to those they have harmed. The community can provide opportunities and guidance for such acts of reparation. Involvement in community service can be a practical way for offenders to demonstrate their commitment to making amends.

4. Teaching Values and Moral Guidance:

Communities often serve as centers of moral and ethical guidance. In the process of atonement, individuals may need guidance on how to live a more virtuous and responsible life. Community members, including religious or moral leaders, can offer valuable insights and support in this regard.

5. Preventing Recidivism:

Community involvement can contribute to preventing recidivism (repeated harmful behavior). By offering a sense of belonging, moral guidance, and practical support, the community can reduce the likelihood of individuals returning to harmful actions. This helps ensure that the process of atonement and redemption is not only a one-time event but a sustainable transformation.

6. Promoting Healing and Restoration:

Atonement is not only about individuals seeking redemption but also about healing the harm caused to victims, the community, and relationships. The community can actively participate in the healing and restoration process by providing a supportive environment for all parties involved.

7. Offering Opportunities for Personal Growth:

The community can create opportunities for personal growth and skill development for individuals seeking atonement. These opportunities can empower them to become productive and responsible members of the community, contributing to their redemption and the well-being of society.

In summary, community involvement is instrumental in the atonement and redemption process. It provides support, accountability, opportunities for reconciliation, moral guidance, and a sense of belonging, which are vital for individuals seeking to make amends for their actions and transform their lives. The community's active role enhances the overall effectiveness of atonement and fosters a sense of healing, reconciliation, and restoration within the community.

CHAPTER 06

RECONCILIATION

Paul's insights into reconciliation, both in terms of human relationships and the broader divine plan of salvation, are deeply relevant to restorative justice.

Reconciliation, as understood in the teachings of the Apostle Paul in the Book of Romans and its role in restorative justice, is a profound and transformative concept. Let's explore Paul's teachings on reconciliation and its significance in restorative justice:

1. Paul's Teachings on Reconciliation:

In the context of Paul's writings, reconciliation primarily refers to the restoration of a harmonious relationship, especially between individuals and God. Key passages in the Book of Romans include:

- Romans 5:10 - "For if, while we were God's enemies, we were reconciled to him through the death of his Son, how much more, having been reconciled, shall we be saved through his life!"

- Romans 5:11 - "Not only is this so, but we also boast in God through our Lord Jesus Christ, through whom we have now received reconciliation."

These verses emphasize that reconciliation with God is made possible through the sacrifice of Jesus Christ. Human reconciliation with God is achieved through faith in Christ's redemptive work.

2. Reconciliation in Restorative Justice:

In restorative justice, reconciliation is a central theme. It involves the restoration of relationships and healing the harm caused by wrongdoing. The connection between Paul's teachings and restorative justice can be seen in the following ways:

- Addressing Harm: Restorative justice aims to address the harm caused by wrongdoing, much like the need for reconciliation in Paul's teachings. Offenders take responsibility for their actions, acknowledging the harm they've caused to victims, communities, and relationships.

- Restoring Broken Relationships: Both Paul's teachings and restorative justice prioritize the restoration of broken relationships. In restorative justice, face-to-face meetings between offenders and victims facilitate dialogue and understanding, leading to reconciliation.

- Community and Support: Paul's writings often emphasize the role of the Christian community in reconciliation. In restorative justice, community involvement plays a crucial role in supporting the atonement and reconciliation process, offering a sense of belonging and guidance.

- Empowering Personal Growth: Reconciliation, as taught by Paul, involves a transformation of individuals. Restorative justice aims to empower personal growth and transformation, offering opportunities for offenders to make amends and develop pro-social behaviors.

3. Healing and Transformation:

Both Paul's teachings and restorative justice emphasize that reconciliation leads to healing and transformation. Reconciliation is not merely a resolution of conflict but a process that results in personal and communal growth. Individuals are restored, relationships are healed, and communities are strengthened.

Reconciliation, as taught by Paul in the Book of Romans, is a central concept in Christian theology. It involves the restoration of a harmonious relationship between individuals and God through faith in Christ's work. In the context of restorative justice, reconciliation extends to the restoration of broken relationships, the healing of harm, and the transformation of individuals and communities. Paul's teachings on reconciliation align with the principles of restorative justice, which seeks to address harm, promote healing, and foster the restoration of individuals and relationships.

An examination of Paul's writings in the Book of Romans and his other epistles reveals the profound concept of reconciliation as understood by Paul and its relevance to restorative justice:

1. Reconciliation in Paul's Teachings:

- Restoration of Relationship with God: For Paul, reconciliation primarily refers to the restoration of a harmonious relationship between humanity and God. He emphasizes that sin has estranged people from God, but through Christ's redemptive work, individuals can be reconciled to God.

- Means of Redemption: In the context of Paul's teachings, reconciliation is closely tied to redemption and atonement. Through faith in Christ and His sacrifice, individuals can be justified, forgiven, and reconciled with God.

-Peace and Unity: Paul often underscores the role of reconciliation in bringing peace and unity. Reconciliation is about making amends and restoring the disrupted relationship with God, as well as promoting unity among believers.

- Transformation and Sanctification: Reconciliation, according to Paul, initiates a transformative process. It leads to personal growth, sanctification, and a change in character, reflecting Christ's image.

2. Reconciliation and Restorative Justice:

- Addressing Harm: The concept of reconciliation in Paul's teachings aligns with the foundational principles of restorative justice. Both emphasize the importance of addressing harm. In restorative justice, this harm may involve victims, communities, or relationships, while in Paul's context, it involves estrangement from God.

- Restoring Relationships: Paul's teachings on reconciliation have parallels with restorative justice's goal of restoring relationships. In restorative justice practices, offenders and victims are given the opportunity to reconcile and repair the harm caused, fostering understanding and forgiveness.

- Community and Support: Both Paul's teachings and restorative justice acknowledge the significance of community and support. In Paul's writings, the Christian community plays a vital role in the reconciliation process. Similarly, restorative justice often involves community participation, providing support to both victims and offenders.

- Healing and Transformation: The ultimate aim of reconciliation, according to Paul, is healing and transformation. It is not just about resolving conflict but about personal and communal growth. Restorative justice shares this goal by offering opportunities for personal development and transformation for offenders.

Paul's teachings on reconciliation in the context of the Book of Romans and his epistles emphasize the restoration of a harmonious relationship between individuals and God through faith in Christ's work. This concept aligns with the principles of restorative justice, which seek to address harm, promote healing, and foster the restoration of individuals and relationships. Both Paul's teachings and restorative justice share a vision of reconciliation that leads to personal and communal transformation.

Reconciliation in human relationships, as understood through Paul's teachings, involves the restoration of harmony and the resolution of conflicts between individuals and communities. Here's how Paul addresses reconciliation and the principles he advocates for restoring broken relationships and promoting harmony:

1. Reconciliation in Human Relationships:

- Acknowledging Wrongdoing: Paul's teachings emphasize the importance of acknowledging wrongdoing as the first step toward reconciliation. Individuals must recognize their part in conflicts and take responsibility for their actions.

- Forgiveness and Mercy: Paul advocates for forgiveness and extending mercy. Just as God has shown mercy to humanity through Christ, he encourages believers to forgive one another. Forgiveness is a fundamental aspect of reconciliation.

- Communication and Understanding: Open and honest communication are essential for reconciliation. Paul promotes understanding and empathy among individuals in conflict. He encourages active listening and seeking to understand one another's perspectives.

- Making Amends: Making amends and taking practical steps to repair the harm caused is crucial. This may involve restitution or acts of kindness to demonstrate a genuine commitment to reconciliation.

2. Principles for Restoring Broken Relationships and Promoting Harmony:

- Humility: Humility is a foundational principle in Paul's teachings on reconciliation. Humble individuals are more willing to admit their mistakes, seek forgiveness, and work toward restoring relationships.

- Love: Love, in the Christian sense, is a driving force behind reconciliation. Paul emphasizes that love should guide individuals in their interactions, leading to acts of kindness and reconciliation.

- Peace and Unity: Paul underscores the importance of peace and unity within communities. He encourages believers to strive for peace, seek unity, and work together to resolve conflicts and restore harmony.

- Community Support: Community support and involvement play a significant role in Paul's teachings. Fellow believers are encouraged to support one another in the process of reconciliation, providing guidance, prayer, and assistance.

- Spiritual Transformation: Paul's teachings often focus on the transformation of individuals through faith in Christ. A transformed heart and mind can lead to a change in behavior, fostering reconciliation and harmony.

Paul's teachings on reconciliation in human relationships center around principles of acknowledging wrongdoing, extending forgiveness and mercy, open communication, making amends, humility, love, and the pursuit of peace and unity. These principles are not only relevant in the context of Christian faith but also align with the principles of restorative justice, which emphasize healing, understanding, and the restoration of broken relationships in a broader societal context.

Reconciliation with God, as understood through Paul's teachings, is a central concept in Christian theology. It involves the restoration of a harmonious relationship between humanity and God through faith in Christ. This reconciliation is closely related to the concepts of redemption and atonement, as discussed earlier. Here's an exploration of Paul's understanding of reconciliation with God and its relationship to redemption and atonement:

1. Reconciliation with God:

- Estrangement due to Sin: Paul acknowledges that humanity is estranged from God due to sin. Sin has created a separation between humans and the divine, leading to a broken relationship.

- Reconciliation through Christ: Paul teaches that reconciliation with God is made possible through Jesus Christ. Christ's sacrificial death and resurrection provide the means for humanity to be reconciled with God.

- Faith as the Path: Reconciliation with God occurs through faith in Christ. Believers are called to trust in Jesus, acknowledge their need for redemption, and accept the forgiveness and grace offered through Christ's work.

- Forgiveness and Justification: Reconciliation involves forgiveness and justification. Through faith in Christ, believers are forgiven for their sins and declared righteous before God. This forgiveness and justification restore the broken relationship.

2. Relationship to Redemption and Atonement:

- Redemption: The concept of redemption, as discussed in earlier chapters, is closely related to reconciliation. Redemption involves being saved from the consequences of sin. Reconciliation follows redemption because once individuals are redeemed through Christ's sacrifice, they can be reconciled with God.

- Atonement: Atonement involves making amends for wrongdoing and seeking forgiveness. In the context of reconciliation, atonement is achieved through Christ's sacrifice, which serves as the means of atoning for humanity's sins.

Atonement and reconciliation go hand in hand, as reconciliation is the ultimate goal of atonement.

- Harmony and Wholeness: Both redemption and atonement serve to bring about harmony and wholeness in the relationship between individuals and God. Reconciliation completes this process by restoring the harmony that was disrupted by sin.

Paul's understanding of reconciliation with God emphasizes that faith in Christ is the path to restoration. This reconciliation is closely linked to the concepts of redemption and atonement. Redemption through Christ's sacrifice paves the way for reconciliation, and atonement is achieved through Christ's atoning work. The ultimate goal of this reconciliation is to restore the harmonious relationship between humanity and God, emphasizing forgiveness, justification, and grace.

Restorative justice and reconciliation are closely related concepts, and the principles of restorative justice align with Paul's teachings on reconciliation in several ways. Both emphasize healing, understanding, and the restoration of individuals and relationships. Here's how restorative justice practices can facilitate reconciliation in the context of harm caused by wrongdoing, aligning with Paul's teachings:

1. Acknowledging Wrongdoing:

- Restorative Justice: Restorative justice begins with acknowledging the wrongdoing. Offenders are encouraged to take responsibility for their actions, recognizing the harm they've caused.

- Paul's Teachings: Acknowledgment of sin and wrongdoing is a fundamental principle in Paul's teachings on reconciliation. Reconciliation with God starts with acknowledging one's need for redemption and forgiveness.

2. Making Amends:

- Restorative Justice: Restorative justice practices often involve making amends to victims and communities. Offenders are encouraged to take concrete actions to repair the harm they've caused.

- Paul's Teachings: In Paul's writings, reconciliation often involves taking actions that promote harmony and restoration, such as seeking forgiveness and making restitution.

3. Victim-Offender Dialogue:

- Restorative Justice: A central feature of restorative justice is victim-offender dialogue. This process allows victims to express their feelings and concerns while offenders listen, fostering understanding.

- Paul's Teachings: Paul emphasizes empathy and understanding in resolving conflicts. He encourages believers to bear one another's burdens and work toward reconciliation, promoting mutual understanding.

4. Community Involvement:

- Restorative Justice: Community involvement is a vital component of restorative justice. The community often plays a role in supporting victims, providing guidance, and holding offenders accountable.

- Paul's Teachings: In Paul's context, the Christian community has a significant role in reconciliation, offering support, guidance, and encouragement. Believers are called to support one another in the process of restoration.

5. Healing and Transformation:

- Restorative Justice: Restorative justice aims to promote healing for victims and offenders, transforming their lives and relationships. It seeks to address the harm and promote personal growth.

- Paul's Teachings: Paul's teachings also emphasize that reconciliation leads to healing and transformation. Through faith in Christ, individuals are transformed and empowered to live righteous lives.

Restorative justice practices align with Paul's teachings on reconciliation in their focus on acknowledging wrongdoing, making amends, promoting empathy and understanding, involving the community, and fostering healing and transformation. Both approaches emphasize the importance of addressing harm and promoting reconciliation in the context of wrongdoing.

Healing and transformation in the context of restorative justice and Paul's teachings on reconciliation are profound concepts that align in their emphasis on addressing harm, fostering growth, and restoring individuals and communities. Here's how they align and promote the repair of harm and personal growth:

1. Healing:

- Restorative Justice: Restorative justice aims to promote healing for all parties involved, including victims, offenders, and the broader community. Through the acknowledgment of harm and open dialogue, individuals can find emotional and psychological healing.

- Paul's Teachings: Paul's concept of reconciliation includes the idea of healing, not only in the spiritual sense but also in the emotional and relational sense. Reconciliation leads to the healing of broken relationships and the restoration of harmony.

- Alignment: Both restorative justice and Paul's teachings acknowledge that harm can leave emotional and psychological scars. They share a commitment to addressing these wounds and facilitating the healing process.

2. Transformation:

- Restorative Justice: Restorative justice seeks to transform individuals, particularly offenders. Through acknowledging wrongdoing, taking responsibility, and making amends, offenders have an opportunity for personal growth and transformation.

- Paul's Teachings: Paul's writings emphasize the transformative power of reconciliation through faith in Christ. This transformation extends to individuals' character and behavior, aligning with the idea of sanctification.

- Alignment: Both restorative justice and Paul's teachings recognize the potential for positive change. Offenders are encouraged to transform their lives, making amends for their actions, and becoming more responsible and empathetic individuals.

3. Repairing Harm:

- Restorative Justice: A central goal of restorative justice is to repair the harm caused by wrongdoing. Offenders are encouraged to take action to make amends for the harm they've inflicted on victims and communities.

- Paul's Teachings: In Paul's context, reconciliation is about making amends, seeking forgiveness, and working toward the restoration of relationships. This process includes actions aimed at repairing the harm caused by sin.

- Alignment: Both restorative justice and Paul's teachings emphasize the importance of tangible actions to repair the harm caused. They share a commitment to restoring what has been broken and making things right.

4. Personal Growth:

- Restorative Justice: Restorative justice principles, including accountability, responsibility, and empathy, contribute to personal growth for both offenders and victims. It encourages individuals to learn from their mistakes and make better choices in the future.

- Paul's Teachings: Paul's teachings on reconciliation and transformation involve personal growth and sanctification. Believers are called to grow in their faith and become more Christ-like in their character.

- Alignment: Both restorative justice and Paul's teachings align in their emphasis on personal growth. They recognize that individuals have the potential to change and grow, whether it's in the context of justice and harm repair or spiritual transformation.

Healing and transformation in the context of restorative justice and Paul's teachings on reconciliation align in their goals of addressing harm, promoting personal growth, and restoring individuals and communities. Both approaches emphasize the power of acknowledging wrongdoing, making amends, and facilitating healing and growth, whether it's in the context of justice or spiritual reconciliation.

CHAPTER 07

FORGIVENESS AND REPENTANCE

Forgiveness and repentance are fundamental principles in both restorative justice and Christian teachings, including the writings of the Apostle Paul.

Forgiveness and repentance play pivotal roles in the process of restorative justice:

1. Forgiveness:

- Victim-Centered Healing: Forgiveness is a powerful tool for victims in the restorative justice process. It allows them to release the emotional burden of anger and resentment and find healing.

- Restoration of Relationships: Forgiveness can lead to the restoration of relationships. In restorative justice, it often involves the victim forgiving the offender, which can pave the way for reconciliation.

- Empowerment: Forgiving can empower victims by allowing them to take control of their emotional well-being. It's a choice that can lead to emotional freedom.

2. Repentance:

- Acknowledgment of Wrongdoing: Repentance involves offenders taking responsibility for their actions. It's a critical step in the restorative justice process as it shows a genuine desire to make amends.

- Accountability: Repentance holds offenders accountable for their actions. It's not just saying, "I'm sorry," but also taking concrete steps to right the wrongs and avoid repeating the behavior.

- Transformation: Repentance goes beyond remorse; it leads to transformation. Offenders commit to changing their behavior and making amends, which aligns with the restorative justice goal of personal growth and rehabilitation.

In the restorative justice process, victims are often given the opportunity to express their feelings, which can lead to offenders genuinely understanding the harm they've caused. This understanding can encourage sincere repentance. The interplay between forgiveness and repentance allows for the restoration of individuals and relationships, fostering healing and growth. These concepts also align with Christian teachings, including those of the Apostle Paul, who emphasized the importance of forgiveness, repentance, and reconciliation.

Forgiveness and repentance are fundamental principles in both restorative justice and Christian teachings, including the writings of the Apostle Paul, for several important reasons:

1. Healing and Restoration:

- Restorative Justice: Forgiveness and repentance are central to the healing and restoration process. They offer victims and offenders the opportunity to address harm, find emotional and spiritual healing, and work toward the restoration of broken relationships.

- Christian Teachings: In Christian theology, forgiveness and repentance are seen as pathways to spiritual healing and restoration. Believers are encouraged to seek forgiveness from God through repentance and to extend forgiveness to others, promoting reconciliation.

2. Personal Growth and Transformation:

- Restorative Justice: Encouraging offenders to genuinely repent and make amends is an essential component of restorative justice. This process fosters personal growth and transformation, empowering individuals to change their behavior and become responsible members of the community.

- Christian Teachings: Repentance, as emphasized in Christian teachings, involves a profound transformation of the individual. It is a commitment to turning away from wrongdoing and growing in faith and righteousness. Forgiveness and repentance are intrinsically linked to personal growth and sanctification.

3. Reconciliation and Relationships:

- Restorative Justice: The goal of restorative justice is often reconciliation. Forgiveness and repentance enable the repair of damaged relationships, allowing individuals to move forward together in a more harmonious and constructive manner.

- Christian Teachings: Reconciliation is a key theme in the Christian faith, with forgiveness and repentance as essential components of reconciling with God and others. Paul's writings, for instance, stress the importance of believers reconciling with one another and with God through faith in Christ.

4. Accountability and Responsibility:

- Restorative Justice: Both forgiveness and repentance require offenders to take responsibility for their actions. This accountability is a core principle of restorative justice, as it encourages offenders to acknowledge the harm they've caused and make amends.

- Christian Teachings: Accountability is also emphasized in Christian teachings. Repentance involves acknowledging one's sins and seeking God's forgiveness. Believers are held accountable for their actions, and taking responsibility is an integral part of the faith.

5. Compassion and Empathy:

- Restorative Justice: Forgiveness requires victims to empathize with offenders, and repentance involves the expression of genuine remorse. These actions foster understanding and compassion, which are vital for the healing process.

- Christian Teachings: Compassion and empathy are central to the Christian faith. Jesus's teachings emphasize loving one's neighbor and showing compassion even to those who have wronged us. Forgiveness and repentance reflect this compassionate outlook.

Forgiveness and repentance are fundamental principles in both restorative justice and Christian teachings, including the writings of the Apostle Paul, because they promote healing, personal growth, reconciliation, accountability, and a compassionate and empathetic approach to addressing harm and wrongdoing. These principles align in their focus on addressing harm, repairing relationships, and fostering transformation and restoration.

Forgiveness plays a significant role, both in the context of Christian theology and as a reflection of restorative justice principles. Here's an examination of the importance of forgiveness in the Book of Romans, along with Bible verses that highlight how forgiveness can facilitate healing, restore relationships, and promote personal growth:

1. Facilitating Healing:

- Romans 4:7-8 (NIV): "Blessed are those whose transgressions are forgiven, whose sins are covered. Blessed is the one whose sin the Lord will never count against them."

- Romans 5:20-21 (NIV): "But where sin increased, grace increased all the more, so that, just as sin reigned in death, so also grace might reign through righteousness to bring eternal life through Jesus Christ our Lord."

These verses from Romans highlight the concept that forgiveness through God's grace brings healing and a sense of blessedness. Forgiveness covers sins and allows individuals to experience God's grace, which ultimately leads to healing and eternal life.

2. Restoring Relationships:

- Romans 15:7 (NIV): "Accept one another, then, just as Christ accepted you, in order to bring praise to God."

This verse emphasizes the importance of acceptance and forgiveness within the Christian community. Just as Christ accepted believers, they are encouraged to accept one another. This acceptance and forgiveness contribute to the restoration of relationships, which aligns with restorative justice principles.

3. Promoting Personal Growth:

- Romans 12:2 (NIV): "Do not conform to the pattern of this world, but be transformed by the renewing of your mind. Then you will be able to test and approve what God's will is—his good, pleasing and perfect will."

This verse speaks to personal transformation and growth through faith. The process of renewal and transformation, central to Christian teachings, promotes personal growth and aligns with the principles of restorative justice, which aim to rehabilitate offenders and help them grow as individuals.

Forgiveness is not only about divine forgiveness but also about the forgiveness and acceptance believers are called to extend to one another. This forgiveness facilitates healing, restores relationships, and promotes personal growth, aligning with the principles of restorative justice, which emphasize similar goals in addressing harm and wrongdoing.

The power of repentance is a transformative concept that plays a significant role in both Christian theology and the principles of restorative justice. Repentance goes beyond acknowledging wrongdoing; it involves genuine remorse, taking responsibility, and actively seeking to make amends and change one's behavior. Here are Bible references that highlight the meaning and power of repentance in the context of restorative justice:

1. Acknowledging Wrongdoing:

- Romans 3:23 (NIV): "For all have sinned and fall short of the glory of God."

- 2 Corinthians 7:9 (NIV): "Yet now I am happy, not because you were made sorry, but because your sorrow led you to repentance. For you became sorrowful as God intended and so were not harmed in any way by us."

These verses emphasize the acknowledgment of wrongdoing as a starting point. All have sinned, but this acknowledgment is a precursor to genuine repentance. Sorrow over one's actions can lead to repentance, demonstrating the power of remorse.

2. Taking Responsibility:

- Acts 3:19 (NIV): "Repent, then, and turn to God, so that your sins may be wiped out, that times of refreshing may come from the Lord."

Repentance involves turning to God and taking responsibility for one's actions. By doing so, individuals acknowledge their need for forgiveness and change.

3. Making Amends:

- Luke 19:8 (NIV): "But Zacchaeus stood up and said to the Lord, 'Look, Lord! Here and now, I give half of my possessions to the poor, and if I have cheated anybody out of anything, I will pay back four times the amount.'"

The story of Zacchaeus illustrates the transformative power of repentance. He not only acknowledged his wrongdoing but also took concrete steps to make amends for the harm he had caused.

4. Genuine Transformation:

- Romans 12:2 (NIV): "Do not conform to the pattern of this world, but be transformed by the renewing of your mind. Then you will be able to test and approve what God's will is—his good, pleasing and perfect will."

This verse underscores the idea of transformation through the renewing of one's mind. Repentance leads to a change in behavior and character, aligning with the goals of personal growth and rehabilitation in restorative justice.

In both Christian theology and restorative justice, repentance is a powerful process that acknowledges wrongdoing, takes responsibility, makes amends, and leads to genuine transformation. It is a key element in addressing harm, promoting accountability, and facilitating personal growth and restoration.

Forgiveness is a significant theme in the writings of the Apostle Paul, emphasizing the need for believers to forgive one another and seek reconciliation. In Paul's teachings, forgiveness is deeply intertwined with the principles of Christian faith, reconciliation, and love. Here are some key aspects of forgiveness in Paul's writings:

1. Forgiveness Reflects God's Forgiveness:

- Paul frequently emphasizes that believers should forgive one another because they have first been forgiven by God. He encourages believers to imitate God's forgiveness.

- Ephesians 4:32 (NIV): "Be kind and compassionate to one another, forgiving each other, just as in Christ God forgave you."

2. Forgiveness Leads to Reconciliation:

- Paul's teachings stress the role of forgiveness in reconciling relationships. He encourages believers to seek reconciliation and promote unity.

- 2 Corinthians 5:18 (NIV): "All this is from God, who reconciled us to himself through Christ and gave us the ministry of reconciliation."

3. Forgiveness Fosters Love and Unity:

- Paul emphasizes that forgiveness is an essential element in maintaining love and unity within the Christian community. It's a way to preserve the peace and harmony of the church.

- Colossians 3:13 (NIV): "Bear with each other and forgive one another if any of you has a grievance against someone. Forgive as the Lord forgave you."

4. Forgiveness Overcomes Evil with Good:

- Paul's teachings also encourage believers to respond to wrongdoing with forgiveness and kindness. This approach is in line with the principles of restorative justice, emphasizing transformation and healing.

- Romans 12:21 (NIV): "Do not be overcome by evil, but overcome evil with good."

Paul's teachings on forgiveness stress the importance of believers forgiving one another, imitating God's forgiveness, and seeking reconciliation and unity within the Christian community. These principles align with the values of restorative justice, which aim to address harm, promote reconciliation, and encourage personal growth and transformation.

In the context of the Book of Romans and restorative justice, repentance is a crucial element in the process of addressing harm and wrongdoing. Restorative justice practices encourage offenders to genuinely repent, take responsibility for their actions, and make amends, aligning with Paul's teachings on transformation. Here's how this alignment is reflected:

1. Genuine Repentance:

- Romans 2:4 (NIV): "Or do you show contempt for the riches of his kindness, forbearance and patience, not realizing that God's kindness is intended to lead you to repentance?"

This verse from Romans underscores the role of kindness and patience in leading individuals to repentance. In restorative justice, the emphasis is on fostering genuine remorse and acknowledgment of wrongdoing, which is a crucial step toward personal transformation.

2. Taking Responsibility:

- Romans 14:12 (NIV): "So then, each of us will give an account of ourselves to God."

Restorative justice practices often require offenders to take responsibility for their actions and be accountable for the harm they've caused. This aligns with the idea that each person will give an account of themselves, as stated by Paul.

3. Making Amends:

- Romans 13:10 (NIV): "Love does no harm to a neighbor. Therefore, love is the fulfillment of the law."

Restorative justice principles align with the idea that love does no harm to others. Offenders are encouraged to take concrete actions to make amends and fulfill the moral and legal obligations they have violated.

4. Personal Transformation:

- Romans 12:2 (NIV): "Do not conform to the pattern of this world, but be transformed by the renewing of your mind. Then you will be able to test and approve what God's will is—his good, pleasing and perfect will."

Paul's teachings on personal transformation align with the goals of restorative justice. Repentance, in the context of restorative justice, involves a commitment to change one's behavior, make amends, and grow as an individual.

Paul's emphasis on genuine repentance and transformation is closely related to the principles of restorative justice. Both seek to address harm, promote accountability, and facilitate personal growth and rehabilitation. Repentance is a vital component in this process, allowing individuals to acknowledge their wrongdoing, take responsibility, and work toward positive change.

The interplay of forgiveness and repentance is a dynamic process that plays a pivotal role in the context of restorative justice. Together, they contribute to the restoration of individuals and relationships, promoting healing, reconciliation, and personal growth. Here's how the interplay between forgiveness and repentance works:

1. Acknowledgment of Wrongdoing:

- Repentance begins with the acknowledgment of wrongdoing. Offenders recognize the harm they've caused, and this acknowledgment is crucial for the restorative justice process.

- Ephesians 5:13-14 (NIV): "But everything exposed by the light becomes visible, for it is light that makes everything visible. This is why it is said: 'Wake up, sleeper, rise from the dead, and Christ will shine on you.'"

- Forgiveness often follows this acknowledgment. Victims and the community are willing to extend forgiveness when they see genuine remorse and repentance.

2. Taking Responsibility:

- Repentance involves taking responsibility for one's actions. Offenders admit their guilt and express a desire to make amends.

- 2 Corinthians 7:10 (NIV): "Godly sorrow brings repentance that leads to salvation and leaves no regret, but worldly sorrow brings death."

- When offenders take responsibility, they demonstrate their commitment to righting the wrong, which can lead to forgiveness from those they have harmed.

3. Empathy and Compassion:

- Forgiveness requires victims and the community to extend empathy and compassion to the offender. This compassionate response can facilitate the offender's transformation.

- Colossians 3:12-13 (NIV): "Therefore, as God's chosen people, holy and dearly loved, clothe yourselves with compassion, kindness, humility, gentleness and patience. Bear with each other and forgive one another if any of you has a grievance against someone. Forgive as the Lord forgave you."

- The willingness to forgive reflects the same compassion and kindness shown by God. This compassionate response encourages the offender to genuinely change.

4. Restoration and Reconciliation:

- The ultimate goal of the interplay between forgiveness and repentance is the restoration of individuals and relationships. Through the process of repentance, transformation, and forgiveness, broken relationships can be repaired.

- Galatians 6:1 (NIV): "Brothers and sisters, if someone is caught in a sin, you who live by the Spirit should restore that person gently. But watch yourselves, or you also may be tempted."

- The restoration process often includes support, guidance, and accountability to help individuals move forward in a healthy way.

In summary, the interplay of forgiveness and repentance is a dynamic and transformative process in the context of restorative justice. It involves acknowledging wrongdoing, taking responsibility, extending empathy and compassion, and ultimately working toward the restoration of individuals and relationships. This process aligns with Christian teachings and values, emphasizing the power of reconciliation, personal growth, and healing.

The interplay of forgiveness and repentance is a dynamic process that plays a pivotal role in the context of restorative justice. Together, they contribute to the restoration of individuals and relationships, promoting healing, reconciliation, and personal growth. Here's how the interplay between forgiveness and repentance works:

1. Acknowledgment of Wrongdoing:

- Repentance begins with the acknowledgment of wrongdoing. Offenders recognize the harm they've caused, and this acknowledgment is crucial for the restorative justice process.

- Ephesians 5:13-14 (NIV): "But everything exposed by the light becomes visible, for it is light that makes everything visible. This is why it is said: 'Wake up, sleeper, rise from the dead, and Christ will shine on you.'"

- Forgiveness often follows this acknowledgment. Victims and the community are willing to extend forgiveness when they see genuine remorse and repentance.

2. Taking Responsibility:

- Repentance involves taking responsibility for one's actions. Offenders admit their guilt and express a desire to make amends.

- 2 Corinthians 7:10 (NIV): "Godly sorrow brings repentance that leads to salvation and leaves no regret, but worldly sorrow brings death."

- When offenders take responsibility, they demonstrate their commitment to righting the wrong, which can lead to forgiveness from those they have harmed.

3. Empathy and Compassion:

- Forgiveness requires victims and the community to extend empathy and compassion to the offender. This compassionate response can facilitate the offender's transformation.

- Colossians 3:12-13 (NIV): "Therefore, as God's chosen people, holy and dearly loved, clothe yourselves with compassion, kindness, humility, gentleness and patience. Bear with each other and forgive one another if any of you has a grievance against someone. Forgive as the Lord forgave you."

- The willingness to forgive reflects the same compassion and kindness shown by God. This compassionate response encourages the offender to genuinely change.

4. Restoration and Reconciliation:

- The ultimate goal of the interplay between forgiveness and repentance is the restoration of individuals and relationships. Through the process of repentance, transformation, and forgiveness, broken relationships can be repaired.

- Galatians 6:1 (NIV): "Brothers and sisters, if someone is caught in a sin, you who live by the Spirit should restore that person gently. But watch yourselves, or you also may be tempted."

- The restoration process often includes support, guidance, and accountability to help individuals move forward in a healthy way.

In summary, the interplay of forgiveness and repentance is a dynamic and transformative process in the context of restorative justice. It involves acknowledging wrongdoing, taking responsibility, extending empathy and compassion, and ultimately working toward the restoration of individuals and relationships. This process aligns with Christian teachings and values, emphasizing the power of reconciliation, personal growth, and healing.

CHAPTER 08

THE ROLE OF COMMUNITY

Community plays a vital role in the practice of restorative justice, and Paul's writings in Romans offer valuable insights into the significance of community support and involvement.

The role of community is of paramount importance in the context of restorative justice for several reasons:

1. Support and Accountability:

- Community as a Support Network: Communities serve as a vital support network for both victims and offenders. They provide emotional, psychological, and social support, which is crucial for individuals going through the process of addressing harm and healing.

- Community Accountability: Communities hold individuals accountable for their actions. This community-based accountability can be more meaningful and effective in fostering change than punitive measures alone.

2. Facilitating Healing:

- Emotional and Spiritual Healing: Community involvement can contribute to the emotional and spiritual healing of victims and offenders. Being part of a caring community helps individuals feel valued and supported, which aids in the recovery process.

- Promoting Empathy and Understanding: Communities can foster empathy and understanding among their members. When individuals come together to discuss and address wrongdoing, it can lead to greater empathy and compassion.

3. Encouraging Responsibility and Making Amends:

- Community-Based Programs: Restorative justice often involves community-based programs that offer opportunities for offenders to make amends and contribute positively to their communities. This can lead to personal growth and transformation.

- Restoration of Relationships: Communities play a crucial role in facilitating the restoration of relationships. When both victims and offenders are part of the same community, the potential for reconciliation and rebuilding trust is enhanced.

4. Promoting a Sense of Belonging:

- Community as a Source of Belonging: Belonging to a community can give individuals a sense of purpose and belonging, reducing the risk of reoffending. It can be a motivating factor for individuals to change their behavior and become responsible community members.

5. Prevention and Deterrence:

- Community-Based Prevention: Restorative justice within a community can also serve as a preventive measure. By addressing conflicts and harm directly and meaningfully, it can deter future offenses and contribute to a safer and more harmonious community.

In the context of restorative justice, the community refers to the broader social context where individuals live, interact, and share common values. Communities may include neighborhoods, faith-based groups, schools, or any social setting where people come together. Community members can include victims, offenders, families, friends, and other stakeholders. The involvement of this community is instrumental in making the process of restorative justice more effective and impactful. It creates a collaborative, empathetic, and accountable environment where individuals can address harm, promote healing, and work toward personal growth and reconciliation.

The concept of community and communal aspects are intricately interwoven with the principles of restorative justice. Paul's writings in Romans provide valuable insights into the communal nature of addressing harm and wrongdoing. The early Christian community in Rome, as described by Paul, exemplifies how restorative justice practices involve the entire community, emphasizing accountability, support, and reconciliation.

The Christian community in Rome, as outlined in Romans, serves as a model for communal accountability. Paul emphasizes the importance of mutual edification and working towards peace (Romans 14:19). This demonstrates the community's role in guiding individuals to reconcile and make amends for their wrongdoings. The collective commitment to promoting peace and unity underpins the practice of restorative justice, where the community actively participates in holding individuals accountable for their actions.

Community support is another central theme in the Book of Romans. The Christian community is portrayed as a source of emotional and spiritual guidance, especially for those who have been affected by harm. This resonates with the principle of community support in restorative justice, where victims and offenders receive the empathy and encouragement they need to heal and reconcile. Paul's teachings highlight the Christian community's role as a compassionate and understanding environment, essential for the restoration of individuals.

The early Christian community in Rome played an active role in facilitating reconciliation. Paul's exhortation to "accept one another, just as Christ accepted you" (*Romans 15:7*) reinforces the idea of the community as an agent of reconciliation. This aligns with restorative justice practices that emphasize the importance of community involvement in resolving conflicts and rebuilding relationships. The community's acceptance and willingness to promote unity contribute to the restoration process.

The principles of transformation and renewal are also central to the communal aspects depicted in Romans. The Christian community is encouraged not to conform to the patterns of the world but to be transformed by the renewing of the mind (Romans 12:2). This underscores the community's role in promoting personal growth and rehabilitation, mirroring the restorative justice aim of helping individuals change and reintegrate into society. In the Book of Romans, the Christian community acts as a catalyst for personal transformation, aligning with the principles of restorative justice that seek to rehabilitate and restore individuals within a supportive community framework.

Community plays a vital role in the practice of restorative justice, and Paul's writings in Romans offer valuable insights into the significance of community support and involvement for several reasons:

1. Accountability and Responsibility:

- In restorative justice, community members play a pivotal role in holding individuals accountable for their actions. Paul's writings in Romans underscore the idea of mutual accountability and support within the Christian community.

- Paul encourages the community to "bear with each other" (Colossians 3:13), highlighting the need for communal support in addressing harm and wrongdoing.

2. Emotional and Spiritual Healing:

- Communities provide the emotional and spiritual support necessary for healing, both for victims and offenders. Paul's teachings reflect the role of the Christian community in offering emotional guidance.

- The Christian community in Rome, as described by Paul, serves as a source of comfort, empathy, and mutual edification, which aligns with the emotional and spiritual healing aspects of restorative justice.

3. Facilitating Reconciliation:

- Restorative justice emphasizes reconciliation between individuals, which is often initiated and facilitated by the community. Paul's teachings encourage acceptance and unity within the community, underscoring the importance of reconciliation.

- Paul's message of "accept one another, just as Christ accepted you" (Romans 15:7) resonates with the restorative justice practice of promoting unity and repairing relationships.

4. Personal Transformation:

- Paul's writings in Romans emphasize personal transformation and renewal within the Christian community. The community is a catalyst for individual growth and rehabilitation.

- Restorative justice aims to facilitate personal growth and transformation in offenders. The role of the community in supporting this transformation aligns with Paul's teachings on renewal.

Community support and involvement are fundamental in restorative justice, as they foster accountability, promote emotional and spiritual healing, facilitate reconciliation, and contribute to personal transformation. Paul's writings in Romans provide a biblical foundation for these principles, highlighting the essential role of the Christian community in addressing harm and wrongdoing and promoting reconciliation and restoration.

Community-based accountability is a fundamental concept within restorative justice, and it's exemplified by the Christian community in Rome, as described in the Book of Romans. This form of accountability focuses on mutual support, reconciliation, and the restoration of individuals who have committed wrongdoing.

The verse from Romans 14:19, "Let us therefore make every effort to do what leads to peace and to mutual edification," reflects the essence of community-based accountability. Here's how it works:

1. Mutual Accountability: In the Christian community in Rome, as in restorative justice, community members hold each other accountable for their actions. They work together to encourage individuals to take responsibility for their wrongdoing.

2. Promoting Peace: The primary goal of community-based accountability is to promote peace within the community. This peace is not merely the absence of conflict but the presence of reconciliation and harmony.

3. Restoration and Mutual Edification: Community members strive for mutual edification, which means they support and build up one another. This support includes helping those who have committed wrongdoing find a path toward restoration.

4. Emphasis on Growth: Community-based accountability focuses on the personal growth and transformation of individuals. It recognizes that accountability should lead to positive change and the avoidance of future harm.

Overall, community-based accountability, as reflected in the Christian community in Rome and supported by Romans 14:19, emphasizes the responsibility of the community to guide individuals toward taking ownership of their actions, promoting peace, and working collectively for mutual edification and restoration. This aligns closely with the principles of restorative justice, where the community plays an active role in holding individuals accountable for their actions and supporting their journey toward reconciliation and personal growth.

Community serves as a vital support system in resolving conflicts for several compelling reasons:

1. Emotional and Spiritual Guidance:

- Community support offers emotional and spiritual guidance, which is essential for individuals involved in conflicts. Victims and offenders often experience a range of emotions, including anger, grief, and remorse. The community provides a safe space for them to express these emotions, seek solace, and find spiritual comfort.

2. Encouragement and Empathy:

- In conflicts, individuals may feel isolated and overwhelmed. Community members, inspired by passages such as Romans 15:1, "We who are strong ought to bear with the failings of the weak," provide encouragement and empathy. They bear the burdens of those affected and offer a listening ear.

3. Moral and Ethical Framework:

- Communities often have shared moral and ethical values that can guide individuals in conflict. These shared values are the foundation of many restorative justice practices, emphasizing the importance of making amends and seeking reconciliation.

4. Promoting Reconciliation:

- Community support aligns with the goals of reconciliation in conflict resolution. When both victims and offenders are part of the same community, there is a better chance of fostering understanding and healing, ultimately leading to reconciliation and a sense of unity.

5. Personal Growth and Rehabilitation:

- The community helps individuals involved in conflicts grow and rehabilitate. By offering support, guidance, and accountability, it aids in the process of personal transformation, which is crucial in restorative justice.

6. Building Trust:

- Trust is vital in resolving conflicts, and community support plays a significant role in rebuilding trust between conflicting parties. When community members act as mediators and sources of support, they contribute to the process of restoring trust.

In light of Romans 15:1, the community serves as a source of strength and support for those involved in conflicts. It encourages the strong to bear with the weaknesses of others and not focus solely on self-interest. The willingness of the community to come together to offer support and guidance is instrumental in resolving conflicts, promoting healing, and fostering reconciliation.

Community-led reconciliation is a powerful aspect of restorative justice where the community actively participates in facilitating the reconciliation process between individuals involved in conflicts. The community, inspired by passages like Romans 15:7, "Accept one another, then, just as Christ accepted you, in order to bring praise to God," plays a central role in fostering unity, forgiveness, and restoration. Here's how it works:

1. Encouraging Acceptance: The community embraces the principle of acceptance, mirroring the acceptance of Christ. This acceptance is essential for individuals to find the courage to forgive and be forgiven. When the community leads by example, it creates

an atmosphere of grace and compassion that can encourage those in conflict to accept each other.

2. Promoting Forgiveness: Community members actively encourage the forgiveness process. They exemplify the forgiving nature of Christ and demonstrate that forgiveness is not a sign of weakness but a powerful path to healing and reconciliation. Their support makes it easier for individuals to embrace the idea of forgiveness.

3. Rebuilding Unity: Unity is a key goal of community-led reconciliation. By working together to mend broken relationships and resolve conflicts, the community helps rebuild a sense of unity among individuals who were once in conflict. This unity promotes harmony and cooperation within the community.

4. Accountability and Support: The community provides both accountability and support to those involved in conflicts. It holds individuals responsible for their actions, ensuring that amends are made, and it offers emotional and practical support for those seeking to reconcile.

5. Bringing Praise to God: The ultimate aim, as expressed in Romans 15:7, is to bring praise to God through the reconciliation process. By leading reconciliation efforts, the community demonstrates the transformative power of forgiveness and healing, reflecting the grace and love of God.

Community-led reconciliation is a powerful and transformative aspect of restorative justice. It emphasizes the role of the community in actively participating in conflict resolution, promoting acceptance, forgiveness, unity, and accountability. Through their actions, community members contribute to the restoration of individuals and relationships, ultimately fulfilling the biblical principle of bringing praise to God through the practice of reconciliation.

Community-based restoration programs are initiatives that engage the community in the process of restoring individuals who have committed wrongdoings and resolving conflicts. These programs align with restorative justice principles and are essential for several reasons:

1. Promoting Responsibility: Community-based restoration programs provide individuals with opportunities to take responsibility for their actions. This aligns with the restorative justice principle that accountability is a crucial step in addressing harm and promoting personal growth and transformation.

2. Encouraging Transformation: The renewal of the mind, as mentioned in Romans 12:2, is a central theme in both early Christian communities and modern restorative justice programs. These programs aim to transform the mindset of individuals involved in conflicts, helping them understand the consequences of their actions and encouraging them to change for the better.

3. Providing Support and Guidance: Community-based restoration programs often offer support and guidance for both victims and offenders. They create a safe and empathetic space where individuals can share their experiences, emotions, and stories. This support is crucial for emotional healing and reconciliation.

4. Rebuilding Trust: Restorative justice, as well as community-based programs, emphasizes rebuilding trust. Trust is a

cornerstone of any healthy community, and these programs work toward restoring trust between conflicting parties.

5. Preventing Recidivism: By addressing conflicts and harm directly and promoting personal growth and transformation, community-based restoration programs reduce the likelihood of reoffending. They focus on addressing the root causes of wrongdoing and preventing future harm.

6. Fostering Community Engagement: These programs foster community engagement and active participation in the reconciliation process. When the community is directly involved in restoring individuals and relationships, it strengthens community bonds and cohesion.

7. Reflecting Biblical Values: The principles of personal growth, transformation, renewal, and accountability align with the biblical values reflected in Romans 12:2. These values are at the core of early Christian communities and are also integral to modern community-based restorative justice programs.

Community-based restoration programs are vital because they actively involve the community in addressing harm and conflict resolution, promoting personal growth, and encouraging transformation. These programs align with the principles of restorative justice, reflecting biblical values and working toward the renewal of individuals and the community as a whole. They play an essential role in fostering accountability, reconciliation, and the prevention of future harm.

The integral role of the community in the restorative justice process, as reflected in the Book of Romans, serves as an inspirational model for contemporary community-based restorative justice initiatives. Here's how the principles from the Book of Romans can inform and inspire these modern initiatives:

1. Accountability and Responsibility:

- The Book of Romans emphasizes mutual accountability and bearing with one another's failings. This principle can inspire community-based restorative justice programs to actively involve the community in holding individuals accountable for their actions.

2. Emotional and Spiritual Support:

- The Christian community in Rome provided emotional and spiritual support, which aligns with the need for emotional healing in modern restorative justice. Community-based initiatives can draw from this principle to create supportive environments for victims and offenders.

3. Facilitating Reconciliation:

- Romans highlights the role of the community in facilitating reconciliation and promoting unity. This can inspire modern programs to engage the community in actively working towards conflict resolution and fostering a sense of unity among individuals.

4. Personal Transformation:

- The community's role in promoting personal transformation and renewal, as found in Romans, can encourage contemporary initiatives to focus on the rehabilitation and growth of individuals involved in conflicts.

5. Rebuilding Trust:

- Trust is essential in both the Book of Romans and modern restorative justice. The Book of Romans reflects the community's role in rebuilding trust, a principle that can guide today's programs in restoring trust between conflicting parties.

6. Prevention of Recidivism:

- By addressing the root causes of wrongdoing and preventing reoffending, community-based programs can embrace the principle of prevention found in Romans.

7. Community Engagement:

- The community's active participation in the reconciliation process, as shown in Romans, encourages modern initiatives to foster community engagement. Involving the community creates a sense of ownership and shared responsibility.

8. Reflecting Biblical Values:

- Modern community-based restorative justice initiatives can draw inspiration from the biblical values reflected in the Book of Romans. By aligning their practices with these values, they can create programs that reflect compassion, grace, and the pursuit of unity and reconciliation.

Incorporating these principles from the Book of Romans, contemporary community-based restorative justice initiatives can offer more holistic and effective approaches to addressing harm and resolving conflicts. By involving the community, they can tap into a powerful source of support, accountability, and healing, ultimately fostering personal growth, reconciliation, and the prevention of future harm.

CHAPTER 09

RESTITUTION AND REPAIR

In the Book of Romans, the concept of restitution and making amends is foundational for understanding the restorative justice approach to addressing harm and wrongdoing. This concept is deeply rooted in the principles of biblical justice and is reflected in various passages throughout Romans.

Restitution and repair are fundamental concepts within the context of restorative justice. They involve actions taken by an offender to address the harm they have caused to victims and the community. Here's a breakdown of these concepts:

1. Restitution:

- Restitution refers to the act of compensating victims for the tangible losses or damages they have suffered as a result of an offense. It involves the offender making financial or material amends to the victim.

- Restitution aims to make victims whole again by reimbursing them for any financial losses they have incurred due to the offense. It can cover expenses such as medical bills, property damage, or stolen items.

- Restitution is a way for offenders to take direct responsibility for the harm they've caused and to demonstrate a commitment to making things right.

2. Repair:

- Repair, in the context of restorative justice, goes beyond financial compensation. It encompasses a broader range of actions taken by offenders to address the harm they have caused.

- Repair may involve sincere apologies, efforts to mend broken relationships, community service, or any actions that contribute positively to the affected individuals or the community.

- The goal of repair is to restore not only the tangible losses but also the emotional and social well-being of victims and the community. It focuses on healing and reconciliation.

In essence, both restitution and repair are about taking responsibility for one's actions, acknowledging the harm caused, and actively working to make amends. Restitution primarily deals with financial compensation, while repair encompasses a wider range of actions that promote healing and reconciliation. These concepts are integral to the restorative justice approach, which aims to address harm and wrongdoing by involving all affected parties and focusing on accountability and restoration.

In the Book of Romans, the concept of restitution and making amends is foundational for understanding the restorative justice approach to addressing harm and wrongdoing. Romans offers profound insights into the principles that underlie restorative justice, emphasizing the importance of accountability, reconciliation, and personal transformation.

First and foremost, Romans underscores the biblical principle of personal responsibility. The idea that each individual is accountable for their actions aligns closely with restorative justice, which places a strong emphasis on offenders taking ownership of their wrongdoing. By acknowledging their actions and the harm they've caused, offenders can begin the process of making amends.

Additionally, the Book of Romans promotes reconciliation as a central theme. Making amends and restitution are intrinsically tied to the concept of reconciliation. Romans encourages individuals to seek peace and unity, mirroring restorative justice's goal of repairing harm and restoring relationships between victims and offenders.

Furthermore, the transformative power of faith and renewal found in Romans is essential to the restorative justice process. Making amends is not merely about external actions but also about the internal transformation of offenders. Romans teaches that true change comes from a renewed mind and heart, a concept that resonates with the restorative justice approach, which seeks to guide offenders toward personal growth and positive change.

The Book of Romans offers a biblical foundation for the principles of restitution and making amends, which are integral to the restorative justice approach. These concepts are rooted in personal responsibility, the pursuit of reconciliation, and the transformative power of faith and renewal. Understanding Romans in this context provides valuable insights into how restorative justice can address harm and wrongdoing while emphasizing accountability, healing, and the restoration of individuals and communities.

Acknowledging wrongs is imperative in restorative justice processes for several compelling reasons:

1. Accountability: Acknowledging one's wrongdoings is the first step in taking personal responsibility for one's actions. In restorative justice, offenders are encouraged to admit to their mistakes and accept that they have caused harm. This accountability is essential for addressing the consequences of the offense.

2. Empathy and Understanding: Acknowledgment allows offenders to understand the impact of their actions on victims and the community. It fosters empathy and an appreciation of the suffering and trauma experienced by those harmed. This understanding is a foundation for genuine remorse.

3. Victim-Centered Approach: Restorative justice places victims at the center of the process. When offenders acknowledge their wrongs, it validates the experiences of victims and acknowledges the harm they have endured. This validation is crucial for victims' healing and recovery.

4. Conflict Resolution: Acknowledgment paves the way for effective conflict resolution. It creates an environment where open and honest communication can occur between victims and offenders. This, in turn, supports the reconciliation process and helps both parties move toward a resolution.

5. Preventing Recidivism: By acknowledging their wrongs and taking responsibility, offenders are more likely to commit to

personal growth and behavior change. This commitment can be a significant factor in preventing recidivism and future harm.

6. Restoration of Dignity: Acknowledgment is a way of affirming the inherent worth and dignity of all parties involved in the restorative justice process. It acknowledges that every individual deserves respect, compassion, and the opportunity for redemption.

7. Promoting Healing: For both victims and offenders, acknowledgment is a crucial component of the healing process. It provides a sense of closure and allows individuals to move forward with the assurance that their voices have been heard.

In essence, acknowledging wrongs is not just a formality; it is the cornerstone of the restorative justice process. It sets the stage for accountability, empathy, victim-centeredness, conflict resolution, and personal growth, ultimately leading to the restoration of individuals and communities affected by harm and wrongdoing. Romans' emphasis on acknowledgment aligns with these principles, highlighting the importance of recognizing one's own wrongdoing as a significant step toward reconciliation and justice.

Taking responsibility is of paramount importance in restorative justice decision-making for various reasons:

1. Accountability: Restorative justice places a strong emphasis on personal accountability. By taking responsibility for their actions, offenders acknowledge their wrongdoing and the harm caused. This accountability is integral to addressing the consequences of the offense and promoting justice.

2. Ownership of Behavior: Taking responsibility means recognizing one's role in causing harm. This acknowledgment is a fundamental step in understanding the impact of one's actions on victims and the community. It's an essential element in accepting that one has transgressed societal norms and values.

3. Rebuilding Trust: Personal responsibility is a key factor in rebuilding trust between victims and offenders. When offenders take ownership of their actions and demonstrate genuine remorse, it can lead to the restoration of trust. This trust is crucial in the reconciliation process.

4. Empowerment of Victims: Restorative justice empowers victims by allowing them to have a voice in the process. When offenders take responsibility, it validates victims' experiences and acknowledges the harm they've endured. This empowerment is central to the healing and recovery of victims.

5. Commitment to Change: Taking responsibility is not merely an acknowledgment but also a commitment to change one's behavior. It signals a willingness to make amends, contribute positively to the community, and prevent future harm. This commitment aligns with restorative justice's goals of personal growth and transformation.

6. Personal Growth: Restorative justice encourages personal growth and development for offenders. By taking responsibility for their actions, individuals can engage in the process of self-reflection and growth. They learn from their mistakes and commit to leading more responsible and ethical lives.

In essence, taking responsibility is a cornerstone of restorative justice decision-making. It is a powerful way to address harm and wrongdoing while emphasizing accountability, reconciliation, and the personal growth of individuals involved. This principle aligns with Romans' encouragement to take responsibility for one's behavior and its consequences, ultimately reflecting a commitment to personal and communal healing.

Repairing harm is a critical concept within the context of restorative justice. It involves taking practical actions to address the damage, suffering, and negative consequences caused by an offense. Repairing harm can include several elements:

1. Compensating Victims: One aspect of repairing harm is compensating victims for their losses. This compensation may take the form of financial restitution, covering costs like medical expenses, property damage, or stolen items. It aims to make victims whole by reimbursing them for tangible losses.

2. Restoring Relationships: Repairing harm also focuses on restoring relationships between victims and offenders. This may involve sincere apologies, acknowledging the pain and suffering caused, and working toward reconciliation. Restoring relationships is integral to the healing process for both parties.

3. Community Service: Offenders may engage in community service as a means of repairing harm. By giving back to the community, they contribute positively and demonstrate their commitment to making amends. Community service benefits not only the community but also the offenders by helping them become responsible and contributing members of society.

4. Promoting Personal Growth: Repairing harm often includes measures that encourage the personal growth and

transformation of offenders. This can involve educational programs, counseling, or rehabilitation efforts to address the underlying causes of the offense and prevent reoffending.

The importance of repairing harm, as emphasized in Romans and reflected in restorative justice principles, cannot be overstated. Here's why it is significant:

1. Restoration: Repairing harm is essential for restoring what has been broken. It helps victims find closure and enables both victims and offenders to move forward. It promotes the healing and recovery of individuals and communities affected by harm.

2. Accountability: Repairing harm demonstrates a commitment to accountability. It shows that offenders are taking responsibility for their actions and are willing to take concrete steps to address the consequences.

3. Reconciliation: Repairing harm contributes to the process of reconciliation. By making genuine efforts to repair the harm, offenders can rebuild trust and mend relationships, ultimately promoting harmony and unity.

4. Prevention of Recidivism: Repairing harm by promoting personal growth and transformation is a key factor in preventing reoffending. It offers offenders a chance to learn from their mistakes and become more responsible members of society.

5. Promoting a Positive Community: Engaging in community service and making amends positively contributes to the well-being of the community. It fosters a sense of community cohesion and demonstrates that individuals can learn from their mistakes and contribute positively to society.

Repairing harm is crucial in both the restorative justice process and as portrayed in Romans. It serves as a means of restoring what has been broken, promoting accountability, reconciliation, personal growth, and community well-being. By making genuine efforts to repair harm, individuals and communities can move toward healing, reconciliation, and a sense of justice.

In the context of restorative justice and as promoted in Romans, the responsibility for seeking reconciliation is shared among multiple parties, and it's a collaborative effort. Here's a breakdown of who holds responsibilities for seeking reconciliation:

1. Offenders: Offenders bear a significant responsibility for seeking reconciliation. They are expected to take ownership of their actions, express genuine remorse, and make meaningful efforts to repair the harm they've caused. This includes acknowledging the impact of their behavior on victims and actively working to make amends. Offenders play a crucial role in demonstrating their commitment to personal transformation and reconciliation.

2. Victims: Victims also have a role in seeking reconciliation. While they are not responsible for the offense, they hold the power to forgive and engage in the reconciliation process. Victims may express their needs, feelings, and expectations regarding the reconciliation process, and their willingness to engage in open and honest communication can facilitate the path to reconciliation.

3. Community and Support Systems: The broader community, including family, friends, and community organizations, can play a supportive role in seeking reconciliation.

They can provide emotional and spiritual guidance to both victims and offenders, offering a network of support that encourages healing and reconciliation.

4. Mediators and Facilitators: In some cases, trained mediators and facilitators may be involved in the reconciliation process. They assist in creating a safe and structured environment for open communication between victims and offenders. Their role is to guide the conversation, promote understanding, and help both parties work towards a resolution.

5. Society as a Whole: Society at large also holds a responsibility for seeking reconciliation. A society that values and supports restorative justice principles fosters an environment where reconciliation is more likely to occur. This involves recognizing the importance of redemption, forgiveness, and the restoration of individuals within the community.

In essence, seeking reconciliation is a collective effort that involves offenders, victims, the community, mediators, and society as a whole. It's a shared responsibility that requires open communication, understanding, and a commitment to addressing harm and restoring relationships. Romans' emphasis on reconciliation aligns with these principles, highlighting the collaborative nature of the reconciliation process within the context of restorative justice.

Transformation and renewal, as emphasized in the Book of Romans and many Christian teachings, are central themes within the Christian faith. They revolve around the idea of profound personal change and spiritual renewal through faith in Christ. Here's why the Book of Romans underscores these concepts and their relevance to the process of making amends and reconciliation:

1. Spiritual Transformation: The Book of Romans emphasizes that faith in Christ can bring about a spiritual transformation in an individual's life. This transformation involves a deep change in one's beliefs, values, and character. It is seen as a renewal of the inner self, aligning one's life with the teachings and values of Christ.

2. Moral Renewal: Personal transformation also extends to one's behavior and moral character. Romans teaches that faith in Christ leads to a renewal of the mind, which, in turn, impacts one's actions. This moral renewal is crucial in the context of making amends because it signifies a genuine commitment to changing one's behavior and making positive contributions to society.

3. Commitment to Righteousness: Romans underscores the pursuit of righteousness as a result of faith in Christ. This pursuit involves a dedication to living a just and righteous life. In the context of making amends, a commitment to righteousness is essential as it aligns with the principles of restorative justice, which emphasize accountability and taking positive actions to repair harm.

4. Healing and Reconciliation: The transformation and renewal emphasized in Romans also contribute to healing and reconciliation. When offenders undergo a personal transformation and commit to renewing their lives through faith, it paves the way for reconciliation with victims. This transformation can lead to the rebuilding of trust and the restoration of relationships.

5. Personal Growth and Contribution: Transformation and renewal are not only about personal change but also about contributing positively to society. In the process of making amends, offenders are encouraged to be agents of positive change within their communities. Romans' emphasis on transformation supports this commitment to personal growth and community contributions.

The Book of Romans emphasizes personal transformation and renewal through faith in Christ because it is seen as the path to spiritual and moral renewal, a commitment to righteousness, and the healing and reconciliation of individuals and communities. These themes align with the principles of making amends in restorative justice, where personal transformation is a crucial aspect of repairing harm, promoting reconciliation, and pursuing justice.

Restoring dignity, as reflected in the teachings of the Apostle Paul and aligned with restorative justice principles, is a concept that emphasizes the inherent worth and value of every individual, both victims and offenders. Here are some key points with relevant Bible references:

1. Respecting Human Dignity: The Apostle Paul's teachings, as well as the broader Christian tradition, underscore the fundamental principle of respecting the dignity of every human being. Romans 2:11 (NIV) states, "For God does not show favoritism." This verse reflects the idea that God's justice is impartial and values the dignity of all individuals equally.

2. Forgiveness and Reconciliation: Restoring dignity involves facilitating forgiveness and reconciliation. Romans 12:18 (NIV) encourages individuals to "live at peace with everyone." This

teaching promotes the restoration of relationships, which is essential for rebuilding the dignity of both victims and offenders.

3. Emphasizing Redemption: The concept of redemption is central to the Apostle Paul's teachings. Romans 3:24 (NIV) states, "and all are justified freely by his grace through the redemption that came by Christ Jesus." Redemption is about restoring individuals to a state of grace and dignity, emphasizing the possibility of personal transformation and renewal.

4. The Worth of All Individuals: Romans underscores that every individual has worth in the eyes of God. Romans 5:8 (NIV) explains, "But God demonstrates his own love for us in this: While we were still sinners, Christ died for us." This verse emphasizes that even in a state of sin, individuals are valued and loved by God.

5. Restoring Brokenness: The teachings of the Apostle Paul encourage believers to help restore those who have fallen into sin. Galatians 6:1 (NIV) states, "Brothers and sisters, if someone is caught in a sin, you who live by the Spirit should restore that person gently." This restoration is a process of rebuilding dignity and offering individuals a chance for renewal.

In the context of restorative justice, the concept of restoring dignity aligns with the focus on the inherent worth of all parties involved. Making amends and facilitating reconciliation in cases of harm and wrongdoing is not just about restitution; it's about recognizing the dignity of every individual and valuing their potential for personal growth and transformation. By adhering to these principles, restorative justice aims to repair harm, promote reconciliation, and honor the inherent worth and dignity of everyone affected by wrongdoing.

The Book of Romans offers a robust theological foundation for the concepts of restitution and making amends within the context of restorative justice. At its core, Romans emphasizes the need for acknowledging wrongdoing and personal responsibility. Romans 3:23 (NIV) declares, "For all have sinned and fall short of the glory of God." This recognition of universal sin serves as a starting point for the process of restitution and making amends. It underscores that every individual, regardless of their actions, possesses inherent worth.

Acknowledgment of wrongdoing is only the beginning, as Romans also teaches the importance of personal transformation through faith in Christ. Romans 12:2 (NIV) instructs, "Do not conform to the pattern of this world but be transformed by the renewing of your mind." This transformation is integral to the process of making amends, as it signifies a commitment to change one's behavior and contribute positively to society.

Moreover, the Book of Romans underscores the value of reconciliation and healing. Romans 12:18 (NIV) encourages believers to "live at peace with everyone." This teaching highlights the need for repairing harm and restoring relationships. In the context of restorative justice, restitution is not limited to financial compensation; it extends to the restoration of dignity through genuine reconciliation.

Restitution and making amends, as portrayed in Romans, encompass both the responsibility of offenders to repair the harm they've caused and the readiness of victims to engage in the process of healing and reconciliation. Romans' theological foundation emphasizes that redemption, forgiveness, and the restoration of dignity are not only possible but essential components of the restorative justice journey. By embracing these concepts, individuals can find hope and renewal in the aftermath of wrongdoing, and communities can move towards healing, reconciliation, and justice.

CHAPTER 10

PRACTICAL APPLICATIONS

Practical applications of restorative justice principles, as based on the teachings in the Book of Romans, involve real-life examples and case studies that demonstrate how these principles can be applied in various situations:

1. Community-Based Restorative Justice Programs:

- Case Study: In a community with a history of conflict and division, a restorative justice program was established. It brought together individuals from different backgrounds to engage in open dialogues, acknowledge past wrongs, and work towards reconciliation. As a result, tensions eased, relationships improved, and the community found a path to healing and unity.

2. Victim-Offender Mediation:

- Case Study: In a juvenile justice system, a victim-offender mediation program was implemented for young offenders. Realizing the impact of their actions on victims, these young offenders had face-to-face meetings with those they harmed. Through constructive dialogues, they acknowledged their wrongdoing, expressed genuine remorse, and worked together to develop plans for restitution and personal growth.

3. Restitution and Making Amends:

- Case Study: In a theft case, the offender voluntarily participated in a restitution program. Over time, they diligently repaid the stolen amount to the victim, thus making amends for their actions. The victim, in turn, forgave the offender, and a sense of justice was achieved through this act of restitution.

4. Redemption and Transformation:

- Case Study: An individual with a history of criminal behavior underwent a profound personal transformation through their faith, inspired by the teachings in Romans. They sought reconciliation with those they had wronged and became an advocate for restorative justice in their community, helping other offenders find the path to redemption and renewal.

5. Restoring Dignity:

- Case Study: In a case of workplace harassment, a restorative justice process was initiated. The victim was given an opportunity to express their feelings and needs, and the offender genuinely apologized and committed to making amends. Through this process, the dignity of both parties was restored, and a more respectful workplace culture was established.

6. The Role of the Faith Community:

- Case Study*: A faith community organized a restorative justice conference, where community members and those affected by crime came together to discuss how faith-based principles, rooted in Romans, could be applied to promote reconciliation and healing. This conference led to the creation of support groups and community initiatives centered around restorative justice.

These practical applications illustrate how restorative justice principles, inspired by the teachings in the Book of Romans, can be brought to life in various contexts. These real-life examples and case studies show that restorative justice is not merely a theoretical concept but a powerful approach to addressing harm, promoting reconciliation, and pursuing justice in the real world.

Community-Based Restorative Justice Programs are initiatives that actively engage with the community to address conflicts, repair harm, and promote reconciliation. These programs aim to involve local communities in the process of justice, offering alternatives to traditional punitive approaches. Here are examples of such programs and their impact:

1. Restorative Circles in Schools:

- Program Description: In schools, Restorative Circles are used to address conflicts and misbehavior. Students, teachers, and parents come together to discuss issues, express their feelings, and reach agreements to repair harm.

- Impact: This approach has reduced disciplinary incidents and improved school climate. It empowers students to take responsibility for their actions and promotes a sense of community.

2. Neighborhood Conflict Resolution Centers:

- Program Description: These centers provide a space for community members to resolve disputes, including neighborly conflicts. Trained mediators facilitate dialogues, allowing individuals to discuss issues and reach mutually satisfactory solutions.

- Impact: These centers reduce tensions in neighborhoods, prevent escalation of conflicts, and enhance community cohesion. They empower residents to actively participate in conflict resolution.

3. Victim-Offender Mediation Programs:

- Program Description: These programs bring victims and offenders together in a controlled setting to discuss the impact of the crime, express feelings, and agree on restitution or other means of making amends.

- Impact: Victim-offender mediation programs have been successful in reducing recidivism rates and providing victims with a sense of closure and empowerment. Offenders often gain a deeper understanding of the harm they've caused.

4. Community Sentencing Initiatives:

- Program Description: Community-based sentencing options involve non-violent offenders completing community service or other restorative actions, rather than serving time in jail.

- Impact: These programs reduce incarceration rates and help offenders reintegrate into society. They also allow offenders to directly contribute to their communities, fostering positive change.

5. Faith-Based Restorative Justice Initiatives:

- Program Description: Faith communities often play a role in promoting restorative justice. They host forums, workshops, and support groups that encourage dialogue and reconciliation between victims and offenders.

- Impact: These initiatives provide spiritual guidance and support for individuals affected by crime. They emphasize forgiveness, redemption, and the possibility of transformation through faith.

The impact of community-based restorative justice programs is significant. They empower individuals to actively engage in conflict resolution, provide alternatives to punitive approaches, and foster a sense of ownership and responsibility within communities. Through open dialogue and mutual understanding, these programs contribute to the repair of harm and promote reconciliation, ultimately making communities safer and more cohesive.

Victim-Offender Mediation is a restorative justice process that brings victims and offenders together in a controlled and facilitated setting to discuss the impact of the crime, express their feelings, and agree on restitution or other means of making amends. This approach is aimed at providing both victims and offenders with a voice in the justice process and fostering dialogue to achieve reconciliation. Here are a couple of case studies to illustrate the power of victim-offender mediation:

Case Study 1: Juvenile Offender and Victim of Vandalism

Description: A teenager was arrested for vandalizing a local park, causing significant damage to property. The victim, a community member who regularly used the park, felt violated and angry. Instead of going through a traditional court process, the case was referred to a victim-offender mediation program.

Mediation Process: The teenager and the victim met in a safe and mediated environment. The victim expressed the emotional distress caused by the vandalism, and the offender admitted his wrongdoing and expressed remorse. They discussed the impact on the community and agreed on a plan for the teenager to participate in park cleanup and restoration activities.

Outcome: Through the mediation process, the victim found a sense of closure and satisfaction in the offender's willingness to make amends. The teenager not only contributed to the park's restoration but also gained a deeper understanding of the harm he had caused. The community appreciated this restorative approach, as it allowed them to actively participate in repairing the harm done to their shared space.

Case Study 2: Burglary and the Stolen Heirloom

Description: A home was burglarized, and a valuable family heirloom was stolen. The victim, in this case, had a strong emotional attachment to the stolen item. The offender, who was apprehended, admitted to the crime and expressed a desire to make amends.

Mediation Process: The victim and the offender, along with a trained mediator, engaged in a series of meetings. The victim shared the sentimental value of the stolen heirloom and the emotional distress caused by the burglary. The offender expressed deep remorse and agreed to return the stolen item. In addition, they jointly decided on a plan for the offender to participate in community service.

Outcome: Through the mediation process, the victim not only recovered the stolen heirloom but also witnessed the sincere remorse of the offender. The offender's participation in community service allowed him to demonstrate his commitment to making amends. Both parties found closure and a sense of justice through this facilitated dialogue, highlighting the power of victim-offender mediation in addressing harm and promoting reconciliation.

These case studies illustrate how victim-offender mediation fosters open communication, accountability, and a focus on making amends. This process empowers both victims and offenders to actively participate in resolving conflicts and achieving reconciliation, while also allowing the community to witness and support the restoration of relationships.

Restitution and Making Amends are crucial components of restorative justice, serving several important purposes, including acknowledging responsibility, promoting accountability, and facilitating healing. Here are examples of individuals who have taken these steps as part of their restorative justice journey:

Case Study 1: A Stolen Bicycle and Financial Restitution

Description: A young man stole a bicycle from his neighbor's garage. When caught, he was referred to a restorative justice program. The neighbor, a father of two, felt violated and concerned for his family's safety.

Restitution and Making Amends: In a restorative conference, the young man admitted to the theft and expressed remorse. He agreed to financial restitution to cover the cost of the stolen bicycle and the damage to the neighbor's garage. Additionally, he offered to help the neighbor with household chores as a way to make amends.

Outcome: The financial restitution provided the neighbor with a sense of justice and compensation for his losses. The young man's commitment to making amends by assisting with chores allowed them to rebuild trust and establish a positive neighborly relationship. This process allowed both parties to find closure and healing.

Case Study 2: Embezzlement and Restoring Trust

Description: An employee of a small family-owned business was caught embezzling funds over an extended period. The family, which depended on the business's income, was devastated when they discovered the theft.

Restitution and Making Amends: The employee admitted to the embezzlement and expressed genuine remorse. In a restorative justice conference, they agreed to pay back the embezzled amount, even though it would take several years. Additionally, they offered to provide financial planning advice to help the family secure their financial future.

Outcome: The restitution process allowed the family to recover a significant portion of their losses and plan for their future with confidence. The employee's commitment to repaying the money and offering financial guidance demonstrated a genuine desire to make amends and rebuild trust. Over time, the family forgave the employee, and the business was able to heal and thrive again.

Case Study 3: Community Service for Graffiti Cleanup

Description: A group of teenagers was involved in graffiti vandalism around their neighborhood, causing property damage and distress to residents.

Restitution and Making Amends: Instead of facing criminal charges, the teenagers were referred to a restorative justice program. They agreed to participate in community service, specifically focused on cleaning up the graffiti they had created. They also offered to engage in community discussions about the impact of vandalism on the neighborhood.

Outcome: Through the community service and open dialogues, the teenagers not only physically repaired the harm they had caused but also gained a deeper understanding of the consequences of their actions. The neighborhood appreciated their efforts, and the community became more united in preventing future vandalism.

These case studies illustrate how restitution and making amends are important aspects of the restorative justice process. They offer victims a sense of justice, provide offenders with opportunities to take responsibility, and contribute to the healing and reconciliation of all parties involved. Restitution and making amends go beyond financial compensation; they actively promote personal growth, accountability, and the restoration of trust and dignity within communities.

Redemption and Transformation are integral themes in restorative justice and Christian theology. They involve personal growth, renewal, and the potential for individuals to turn their lives around. Here are examples of individuals who have experienced redemption and transformation through faith and their restorative justice journeys:

Case Study 1: From Drug Addiction to Recovery and Redemption

Description: A man named John struggled with drug addiction for many years, leading to criminal activities, damaged relationships, and a sense of hopelessness.

Redemption and Transformation: John's journey towards redemption began when he sought help for his addiction through a faith-based recovery program. He found strength in his faith, which emphasized the importance of making amends. Over time, he completed rehabilitation, mended relationships with family, and started working as a counselor in the same program that helped him. His transformation from an addict to a counselor inspired others to seek recovery and redemption.

Outcome: John's story became a testament to the power of faith and personal transformation. He not only found redemption but also actively contributed to the recovery and transformation of others. His journey emphasized the potential for individuals to change and become positive influences in their communities.

Case Study 2: A Gang Member's Path to Redemption

Description: Mark was deeply entrenched in a street gang, leading a life of crime, violence, and addiction.

Redemption and Transformation: Mark's transformation began when he found solace in a faith community that emphasized forgiveness, reconciliation, and redemption. He left the gang and started a journey towards recovery. Inspired by his faith, he engaged in victim-offender mediation with individuals he had harmed in the past. Through these dialogues, he expressed remorse, sought forgiveness, and worked on a plan to contribute positively to his community.

Outcome: Mark's transformation from a gang member to a committed advocate for peace and reconciliation was remarkable. He became a mentor to at-risk youth, sharing his own experiences as a testament to the possibility of redemption and personal change. His actions underscored the importance of faith, forgiveness, and second chances in restorative justice.

Case Study 3: From Convict to Community Leader

Description: Susan had served time in prison for a non-violent offense. Upon release, she faced the challenge of rebuilding her life.

Redemption and Transformation: Susan's transformation was deeply rooted in her newfound faith. She became actively involved in her church, which supported her journey toward personal growth and rehabilitation. She sought opportunities to make amends to her family and community. Susan participated in community service, mentoring programs, and restorative justice initiatives, focusing on assisting individuals reintegrating into society.

Outcome: Susan's transformation from a convict to a community leader was inspiring. She offered a living example of redemption and the capacity for individuals to transform their lives positively. Her faith, coupled with her commitment to making amends, allowed her to become a force for good in her community, helping others on their paths to redemption.

These case studies illustrate how redemption and transformation through faith are central to restorative justice. They highlight the potential for individuals to turn their lives around, make amends, and become positive contributors to their communities. Faith often plays a crucial role in these journeys, emphasizing the values of forgiveness, reconciliation, and second chances.

Restoring Dignity is a fundamental aspect of restorative justice, emphasizing the inherent worth and value of every individual involved in the justice process. Here are examples of how restorative justice practices have restored the dignity of both victims and offenders:

Case Study 1: Empowering a Sexual Assault Survivor

Description: A survivor of sexual assault, Sarah, felt a profound loss of dignity and self-worth. She struggled with trauma and sought restorative justice as an alternative to the traditional legal process.

Restoring Dignity: In a restorative justice conference, Sarah had the opportunity to share her experiences and feelings. Her voice was heard, and her pain was acknowledged. The offender expressed genuine remorse and a commitment to making amends. Through this process, Sarah regained a sense of control over her life and found a path to healing. Restorative justice restored her dignity by recognizing her as a person deserving of respect and justice.

Case Study 2: An Offender's Journey to Redemption

Description: Mark, a repeat offender, had spent most of his life in and out of the criminal justice system. He struggled with addiction and a sense of worthlessness.

Restoring Dignity: Mark's journey towards redemption began when he participated in a restorative justice program. Through dialogues with his victims, he expressed remorse, sought forgiveness, and agreed to restitution. The victims and the community saw his commitment to change. Mark's transformation and his active engagement in making amends for his past actions helped him regain his sense of dignity. He was recognized as a person capable of personal growth and redemption.

Case Study 3: Restorative Approaches in a School Setting

Description: In a school, instances of bullying and conflicts among students led to a hostile environment where some students felt their dignity was constantly under threat.

Restoring Dignity: The school implemented restorative justice practices to address conflicts. Students involved in conflicts had the opportunity to discuss their feelings and experiences, allowing them to express their emotions. Through these dialogues, victims and offenders alike found their dignity restored. The focus on repairing harm and rebuilding relationships shifted the school's culture towards one that values the inherent worth and dignity of every student.

Case Study 4: Reintegrating Formerly Incarcerated Individuals

Description: Individuals reentering society after serving time in prison often face challenges related to stigma and the loss of dignity.

Restoring Dignity: Reentry programs that employ restorative justice principles provide support for formerly incarcerated individuals. These programs offer educational opportunities, counseling, and employment assistance. By focusing on personal growth, rehabilitation, and reintegration, they restore the dignity of those seeking to rebuild their lives and contribute positively to society.

These case studies demonstrate how restorative justice practices can restore the dignity of both victims and offenders. By recognizing the inherent worth and value of every individual, restorative justice contributes to personal healing, transformation, and reconciliation. It empowers individuals to regain a sense of self-respect and reestablish their place in their communities.

The role of the faith community is crucial in facilitating restorative justice processes, drawing inspiration from the theological principles found in Romans. Here's why the faith community's involvement is important:

1. Moral and Ethical Guidance: Faith communities often provide a moral and ethical compass based on their religious teachings. The principles of forgiveness, redemption, and reconciliation are deeply ingrained in many faiths, including Christianity. These principles align with the core values of restorative justice. Members of the faith community can offer guidance and support to individuals involved in restorative processes, helping them navigate the moral dimensions of making amends and seeking reconciliation.

2. Emphasis on Healing and Redemption: Faith communities emphasize healing and redemption as essential aspects of a person's spiritual journey. The restorative justice process aligns with these principles by focusing on personal transformation and the potential for individuals to make amends for their wrongdoing. The faith community can encourage individuals to embrace these opportunities for growth, both in their relationship with a higher power and in their relationships with others.

3. Supportive and Nonjudgmental Environment: Faith communities often create a supportive and nonjudgmental

environment where individuals feel safe sharing their experiences and seeking healing. This supportive atmosphere is invaluable for victims, offenders, and their families who are engaged in the restorative justice process. It encourages open communication, fosters empathy, and helps individuals regain a sense of dignity and self-worth.

4. Community Involvement: Faith communities are deeply rooted in their local communities. They can play a pivotal role in building bridges between victims, offenders, and the community at large. By actively engaging their congregations, faith leaders can encourage community participation in restorative justice initiatives, thereby promoting a sense of collective responsibility for healing and reconciliation.

5. Promoting Forgiveness and Reconciliation: The emphasis on forgiveness and reconciliation found in many faith traditions aligns with restorative justice principles. Faith leaders can provide spiritual guidance on forgiveness, assisting individuals in letting go of bitterness and anger. By promoting reconciliation, the faith community can contribute to the repair of relationships and the restoration of harmony within communities.

6. Advocacy and Education: Faith communities can serve as advocates for restorative justice practices, raising awareness of their benefits and advocating for their implementation within the criminal justice system. They can also provide education and training to their members and the broader community about the principles of restorative justice, thereby fostering a greater understanding of its role in repairing harm and promoting healing.

The faith community's involvement in restorative justice processes is essential due to its capacity to provide moral and ethical guidance, emphasize healing and redemption, create supportive environments, mobilize community involvement, promote forgiveness and reconciliation, and advocate for restorative justice. By drawing inspiration from the theological principles found in Romans and other religious texts, faith communities can significantly contribute to the success of restorative justice initiatives.

Restorative justice principles rooted in the Book of Romans can be applied in various situations to promote healing, reconciliation, and personal growth. Here are four key areas where these principles can be beneficial:

1. Criminal Justice: Restorative justice offers a powerful alternative to the punitive aspects of the criminal justice system. By emphasizing the importance of making amends and seeking reconciliation, it can be applied to situations where offenders and victims can engage in dialogue. In cases of non-violent offenses or lesser crimes, restorative processes can help offenders take responsibility for their actions, express remorse, and work towards making amends to victims, their families, and the community. This approach aligns with Romans' teachings on transformation and personal redemption.

2. Community Conflicts: Restorative justice principles can be used to address conflicts within communities. Whether it's disputes between neighbors, tensions in schools, or disagreements in workplaces, the focus on open dialogue, understanding the

impact of actions, and seeking resolution can be highly effective. Restorative processes allow individuals to express their grievances, listen to others, and work together towards healing and reconciliation. These practices promote harmony and unity, echoing the principles of reconciliation in Romans.

3. Family Disputes: In family situations, restorative justice principles can be instrumental in resolving conflicts. Whether it's disputes between parents and children, siblings, or extended family members, restorative approaches encourage communication and understanding. By acknowledging wrongdoing, taking responsibility, and seeking reconciliation, family members can repair damaged relationships. These practices align with Romans' teachings on forgiveness and the importance of familial harmony.

4. School and Education: Restorative justice can be applied effectively in educational settings. It provides a framework for addressing conflicts among students, teachers, and administrators. By focusing on open communication, accountability, and repairing harm, restorative practices can promote a positive school environment where conflicts are resolved constructively. Students can learn the importance of taking responsibility for their actions and working towards reconciliation, fostering an atmosphere of unity and personal growth.

In each of these situations, the principles of restorative justice grounded in the Book of Romans provide a roadmap for addressing harm and conflict in a way that reflects Christian values. By emphasizing personal transformation, accountability, forgiveness, and reconciliation, restorative justice practices promote healing and the restoration of dignity for individuals and communities.

CHAPTER 11

CHALLENGES AND CRITIQUES

While applying restorative justice within a biblical framework, such as the principles found in the Book of Romans, offers numerous benefits, it also faces several challenges and critiques. These issues should be considered when implementing such an approach:

1. Theological Differing Interpretations: One challenge lies in the diverse interpretations of biblical teachings across Christian denominations and faith traditions. Restorative justice principles may not align with every theological perspective. Theological debates can arise over the scriptural basis and interpretation of reconciliation and redemption, potentially hindering the widespread acceptance of restorative justice.

2. Institutional Resistance: The criminal justice system, legal structures, and established correctional institutions are often resistant to significant changes. Implementing restorative justice within these systems can face resistance from those who are comfortable with the current punitive approach. It requires a

substantial shift in mindset and practice, which may be met with skepticism or opposition.

3. Resource Limitations: Restorative justice processes often demand significant resources, including trained facilitators, counselors, and community support. These resources may not always be readily available, making the application of restorative justice challenging, particularly in areas with limited access to such support.

4. Victim and Offender Willingness: The success of restorative justice hinges on the willingness of both victims and offenders to engage in the process. Some victims may be hesitant to face their offenders, fearing retraumatization, and some offenders may not be open to taking responsibility for their actions. The lack of participant willingness can pose a substantial hurdle to effective implementation.

5. Societal Skepticism: Restorative justice challenges the conventional understanding of justice, which often centers on punitive measures. It may face skepticism from the broader society, which may question the efficacy of this approach. Overcoming this skepticism and educating the public about the benefits of restorative justice is a persistent challenge.

6. Ensuring Equity: A significant critique of restorative justice lies in its potential to perpetuate systemic inequities. Critics argue that it may not adequately address structural issues like racism or economic disparities. There is a need for rigorous attention to ensuring that restorative justice processes are equitable and

accessible to all, regardless of social, economic, or racial backgrounds.

7. Measuring Outcomes: Measuring the effectiveness of restorative justice programs and their long-term impact can be challenging. Traditional justice systems often rely on quantitative measures like recidivism rates, whereas the outcomes of restorative justice are multifaceted and may not be easily quantifiable.

8. Lack of Legal Framework: In some jurisdictions, restorative justice may not have a strong legal framework or legislative support. This can lead to inconsistencies in its application and hinder its acceptance and legitimacy.

Addressing these challenges and critiques requires thoughtful planning, robust education, and a commitment to refining restorative justice practices. While not without its difficulties, applying restorative justice within a biblical framework can foster healing and reconciliation, promoting a more compassionate approach to justice.

In the context of the Book of Romans, applying restorative justice within a biblical framework may face certain challenges and critiques:

1. Theological Interpretation: Different Christian denominations and theological perspectives may interpret the teachings of Romans differently. Restorative justice relies on certain theological principles such as reconciliation and redemption, which might not align with every interpretation of the Bible. Disagreements on the scriptural basis and interpretation of these principles can present challenges when attempting to implement restorative justice universally.

2. Resistance to Change: The traditional view of justice in many societies often revolves around punitive measures. Implementing restorative justice within existing legal and correctional systems may encounter resistance from those accustomed to punitive approaches. The shift in mindset and practice required can be met with skepticism and opposition.

3. Resource Limitations: Restorative justice processes demand resources such as trained facilitators, counselors, and community support. These resources may not always be readily available, making it challenging to implement restorative justice, particularly in regions with limited access to such support.

4. Victim and Offender Willingness: The success of restorative justice depends on the willingness of both victims and offenders to participate in the process. Victims may be hesitant to face their offenders, fearing retraumatization, while some offenders may not be open to taking responsibility for their actions. Lack of participant willingness can be a substantial obstacle to effective implementation.

5. Societal Skepticism: Restorative justice challenges the conventional understanding of justice, which is often centered on punitive measures. It may face skepticism from society at large, with questions about its efficacy compared to punitive justice. Overcoming this skepticism and educating the public about the benefits of restorative justice is a persistent challenge.

6. Ensuring Equity: Critics may argue that restorative justice does not adequately address systemic issues like racism or economic disparities. It's essential to ensure that restorative justice

processes are equitable and accessible to all, regardless of social, economic, or racial backgrounds.

7. Legal Framework: In some jurisdictions, restorative justice may lack a robust legal framework or legislative support. This can lead to inconsistencies in its application and hinder its acceptance and legitimacy within the legal system.

Addressing these challenges and critiques in the context of the Book of Romans would require careful consideration, theological dialogue, and a commitment to educating both the faith community and the broader society about the potential benefits of applying restorative justice within a biblical framework.

Theological differing interpretations are challenges that arise due to the diverse ways in which different Christian denominations and faith traditions interpret biblical teachings. These differences can create challenges when applying restorative justice within a biblical framework. Here's why:

1. Doctrinal Variations: Christian denominations and faith traditions may have distinct doctrines and theological beliefs. For example, while one denomination may emphasize certain aspects of redemption and reconciliation, another may have a different theological emphasis. These variations can lead to differing interpretations of biblical passages, including those relevant to restorative justice.

2. Scriptural Emphasis: Different traditions may place varying degrees of emphasis on different sections of the Bible. This means that passages that are central to one denomination's understanding of restorative justice may not hold the same

significance for another. This can result in different interpretations and applications of restorative justice principles.

3. Theological Framework: The theological framework within which a denomination operates can significantly influence their interpretation of biblical principles. For instance, certain traditions may have a strong focus on legal or penal aspects of theology, which could affect their views on justice and reconciliation.

4. Historical Context: The historical context in which a particular denomination or faith tradition was formed can impact its interpretation of biblical passages. Historical events and theological debates throughout the centuries have contributed to the development of specific theological positions.

5. Denominational Leadership: The leadership and theological positions of a particular denomination or faith tradition can also shape its interpretation of biblical texts. The stance of religious authorities within a tradition can influence how certain principles are applied.

6. Interfaith Dialogue: Interfaith dialogue can reveal theological differences among different religious traditions, including those within Christianity. These differences can impact how restorative justice is understood and practiced in interfaith contexts.

Theological debates that stem from these differing interpretations can be a challenge when attempting to apply restorative justice within a biblical framework. It's essential to engage in respectful dialogue and seek common ground while acknowledging that theological diversity is a fundamental aspect of religious pluralism. This diversity can enrich discussions about how to best apply restorative justice principles within a faith context while respecting a wide range of theological perspectives.

Institutional resistance refers to the reluctance or opposition that can be encountered when attempting to introduce significant changes, such as implementing restorative justice, within established systems like the criminal justice system, legal structures, and correctional institutions. Several factors contribute to this resistance:

1. Current Punitive Approach: The traditional approach within many criminal justice systems is primarily punitive, focusing on punishment and retribution as a response to wrongdoing. Those within the system, including law enforcement, legal professionals, and prison authorities, are accustomed to this approach. Introducing restorative justice, which emphasizes reconciliation, restoration, and healing, represents a fundamental departure from this punitive model. This shift challenges the status quo and can face resistance from individuals comfortable with the current approach.

2. Mindset and Culture: The culture within these institutions often reinforces punitive practices. There is a deeply ingrained mindset that revolves around maintaining law and order through punitive measures. This culture can be resistant to change, as it may view restorative justice as a departure from established norms.

3. Skepticism and Opposition: Introducing restorative justice requires a substantial shift in mindset and practice. It challenges deeply rooted beliefs about justice and correctional

practices. Consequently, individuals within the system may be skeptical about the effectiveness of restorative justice, leading to opposition to its implementation. Concerns about its impact on public safety, legal procedures, and institutional practices can further fuel this skepticism.

4. Resource Allocation: Implementing restorative justice often requires additional resources, such as training for personnel, community support, and facilitators. Institutions may resist these additional resource allocations, especially if they perceive restorative justice as a costly endeavor. The allocation of resources can be a contentious issue when proposing this shift.

5. Lack of Awareness: There may be limited awareness and understanding of restorative justice principles within these institutions. This lack of awareness can result in resistance, as individuals may not fully comprehend the potential benefits of adopting a restorative approach.

Overcoming institutional resistance to restorative justice involves a combination of education, training, and collaboration. Efforts to raise awareness about the effectiveness and advantages of restorative justice, as well as providing training for professionals within the system, can help shift the mindset and culture. Building partnerships and coalitions between proponents of restorative justice and key stakeholders within these institutions is also crucial for fostering change. Additionally, highlighting successful case studies and demonstrating the positive outcomes of restorative justice practices can help mitigate skepticism and opposition.

Resource limitations can pose a significant challenge to the effective implementation of restorative justice for several reasons:

1. Trained Facilitators: Restorative justice processes require skilled and trained facilitators who can guide dialogue between victims and offenders. These facilitators play a crucial role in ensuring that the process is fair, respectful, and focused on healing and reconciliation. Training and maintaining a pool of qualified facilitators can be resource-intensive, and it may be challenging to find individuals with the necessary expertise in all regions.

2. Counselors and Support Services: Restorative justice often involves addressing the emotional and psychological needs of victims, offenders, and affected parties. Access to counseling and support services is essential to help individuals cope with trauma, express their feelings, and work towards healing. However, providing these services can strain existing mental health and support resources.

3. Community Support: Engaging the community in restorative justice processes is vital. This requires community members who are willing to participate as volunteers, provide support to victims and offenders, and create a safe space for dialogue. Limited community involvement and support can hinder the application of restorative justice, especially in areas with fewer resources or where community engagement is not readily available.

4. Economic Constraints: Restorative justice programs may need financial resources to operate effectively. This includes funding for administrative costs, facilities, and materials necessary for the process. Economic constraints can limit the ability of

organizations and institutions to establish and maintain restorative justice programs.

5. Geographic Disparities: Resource limitations may be more pronounced in rural or economically disadvantaged areas, where access to trained facilitators, counselors, and community support may be even scarcer. This can result in unequal access to restorative justice services, which goes against the principle of equitable justice.

6. Time and Administrative Costs: Implementing restorative justice takes time and effort, including administrative costs related to case management and coordination. These administrative tasks may require dedicated personnel and financial resources.

Overcoming resource limitations in the application of restorative justice involves a multi-faceted approach. It includes seeking funding and support from government agencies, private organizations, and community partners. Training and capacity-building programs can help develop a pool of skilled facilitators and support personnel. Additionally, exploring innovative approaches, such as online platforms, can help expand access to restorative justice in areas with limited resources. Collaboration among multiple stakeholders, including government agencies, non-profit organizations, and community groups, is essential to address these resource challenges effectively and ensure that restorative justice is accessible to all who can benefit from it.

Victim and offender willingness is vital in the context of restorative justice for several reasons:

1. Voluntary Participation: Restorative justice is based on voluntary participation. Both victims and offenders must willingly choose to engage in the process. This voluntariness is foundational to the principles of empowerment and self-determination. Forcing individuals to participate in restorative justice processes would contradict these principles and could lead to unproductive or even harmful outcomes.

2. Empowerment: Restorative justice aims to empower victims by giving them a voice and a role in the process. For offenders, it offers an opportunity to take responsibility for their actions and make amends. Willing participation ensures that both parties have agency in the process and are actively involved in shaping its outcome.

3. Healing and Recovery: Victims who are not willing to participate may experience further trauma or distress if forced into restorative processes. Their willingness to engage is crucial for the potential healing and recovery that restorative justice can offer. When victims are ready to confront their offenders and seek resolution, they are more likely to experience positive outcomes.

4. Accountability and Responsibility: Offenders who are unwilling to take responsibility for their actions may not genuinely engage in the process. Willingness on the part of the offender is essential for the success of restorative justice. It signifies a sincere commitment to making amends and addressing the harm caused.

5. Outcome Effectiveness: Restorative justice is most effective when participants are genuinely invested in the process and its outcomes. Willing participants are more likely to engage

openly, honestly, and constructively, which can lead to meaningful resolution and reconciliation.

6. Avoiding Re-Traumatization: For victims, particularly in cases of serious harm, the process of facing an offender can be emotionally challenging. Willing participation allows victims to engage at their own pace and when they feel emotionally prepared, minimizing the risk of re-traumatization.

7. Building Trust: The willingness of both victims and offenders to engage in restorative justice can build trust in the process itself. Trust is essential for successful outcomes and for fostering confidence in the broader community in the effectiveness of restorative justice.

To overcome the challenges posed by a lack of participant willingness, practitioners and facilitators must prioritize informed consent and provide support and information to help individuals make the decision that is right for them. Creating a safe and respectful environment that encourages open dialogue and acknowledging the concerns and needs of both victims and offenders are essential steps in ensuring that they willingly participate in restorative justice processes.

Societal skepticism refers to the doubts, reservations, or concerns that the broader society may have regarding a specific concept or approach, in this case, restorative justice. Restorative justice challenges traditional punitive models of justice by emphasizing reconciliation, healing, and community involvement. This shift in focus can lead to skepticism from various segments of society for several reasons:

1. Lack of Familiarity: Restorative justice represents a departure from the familiar punitive model of justice that many people have grown up with. This lack of familiarity can lead to skepticism as individuals may not fully understand the principles and practices of restorative justice.

2. Concerns About Public Safety: Some members of the public may worry that restorative justice places too much emphasis on the needs and rights of offenders, potentially at the expense of public safety. Skepticism can arise from concerns about whether restorative justice adequately addresses public safety issues.

3. Perception of Leniency: Restorative justice is sometimes perceived as being more lenient on offenders compared to traditional punitive measures. This perception can lead to skepticism, especially among those who believe that offenders should face more severe consequences for their actions.

4. Lack of Trust in Offenders: Some individuals may be skeptical of restorative justice's ability to facilitate genuine change and accountability among offenders. They may question whether offenders are willing to take responsibility for their actions and make amends.

5. Misconceptions and Misinformation: Misconceptions and misinformation about restorative justice can contribute to skepticism. This may include misconceptions about what restorative justice entails and its effectiveness in addressing harm and wrongdoing.

6. Cultural and Value Differences: Different cultural and value systems can influence how restorative justice is perceived.

Societal skepticism may be more pronounced in communities or regions where punitive justice is deeply ingrained in the culture.

Overcoming societal skepticism about restorative justice requires proactive efforts to educate the public, dispel myths and misconceptions, and highlight the positive outcomes and benefits of restorative practices. This education can be achieved through public awareness campaigns, community outreach, and the sharing of success stories and case studies that demonstrate the effectiveness of restorative justice in addressing harm, promoting healing, and fostering stronger communities. Additionally, engaging in open and respectful dialogue with skeptics can help address their concerns and provide a more accurate understanding of restorative justice principles and practices.

Ensuring equity in restorative justice is essential for several reasons:

1. Addressing Systemic Inequities: Restorative justice must be mindful of addressing the systemic issues that underlie many forms of harm and wrongdoing. Failing to do so could result in overlooking the root causes of some conflicts, perpetuating inequality, and failing to provide meaningful justice for marginalized communities.

2. Preventing Reinjury: Failing to consider equity in restorative justice processes can risk reinjuring already marginalized individuals or communities. If systemic issues like racism or economic disparities are not addressed, the harm can continue, and individuals or communities may not experience genuine healing and reconciliation.

3. Community Trust and Buy-In: Equity is crucial for building trust and community buy-in for restorative justice programs. Ensuring that these processes are fair and accessible to all members of the community can help foster confidence in the system and its ability to provide just outcomes.

4. Ethical Imperative: There is an ethical imperative to ensure that restorative justice is applied in a just and equitable manner. Equity is a fundamental principle of justice itself, and it is essential for upholding the values of fairness, dignity, and respect for all individuals.

5. Effectiveness: Equity can enhance the effectiveness of restorative justice. Ensuring that marginalized individuals have equal access to and representation in these processes can result in more meaningful resolutions, better compliance with agreements, and stronger community cohesion.

To ensure equity in restorative justice, it is crucial to:

- Address Structural Inequities: Restorative justice programs should acknowledge and actively work to address structural issues like racism, economic disparities, and discrimination that can contribute to harm and wrongdoing.

- Community Engagement: Engage with the affected community and involve them in the design and implementation of restorative justice programs. This helps ensure that the processes are culturally sensitive and relevant.

- Cultural Competency: Provide training to facilitators and practitioners in cultural competency and sensitivity to address the diverse needs of participants.

- Accessible Support: Ensure that individuals, particularly those from marginalized backgrounds, have access to support services to address any emotional, psychological, or material needs they may have.

- Evaluation and Monitoring: Continuously evaluate and monitor the equity of restorative justice programs to identify any disparities and make adjustments as needed.

By prioritizing equity in restorative justice, it becomes a more powerful tool for addressing harm, promoting healing, and fostering stronger, more inclusive communities.

Measuring outcomes in restorative justice is essential for several reasons:

1. Accountability and Transparency: Measuring outcomes ensures that restorative justice programs are held accountable for their effectiveness. This transparency is crucial for maintaining public trust and support.

2. Continuous Improvement: Evaluation and measurement allow for ongoing improvement of restorative justice practices. By understanding what works and what doesn't, practitioners can refine their methods and enhance the quality of services.

3. Evidence-Based Practices: Measuring outcomes provides the opportunity to identify evidence-based practices that have the most positive impact on participants and communities. This can help in refining program models and implementing practices that have proven to be effective.

4. Participant Satisfaction: Understanding participant satisfaction and the perception of fairness is vital. High levels of

participant satisfaction often correlate with successful outcomes, as they indicate that individuals feel their needs and concerns have been adequately addressed.

5. Restitution and Repair: Measuring outcomes helps assess the success of restitution and repair efforts. Evaluating whether offenders have made genuine efforts to make amends for their actions and whether victims have experienced healing and resolution is essential.

6. Community Impact: Restorative justice can have broader community impacts beyond individual cases. Measuring these impacts can help demonstrate the value of restorative justice in building stronger, more cohesive communities.

7. Resource Allocation: Resources are often limited, and measuring outcomes helps in making informed decisions about resource allocation. It ensures that resources are directed toward practices and programs that yield the best results.

8. Policy and Advocacy: Outcomes data can be valuable in advocating for restorative justice at a policy level. It provides evidence of the effectiveness of restorative practices and can be used to advocate for broader implementation and support.

To effectively measure outcomes in restorative justice, it is important to develop appropriate evaluation frameworks and methods. These may include:

- Qualitative and Quantitative Data: A combination of both qualitative and quantitative data can provide a comprehensive view of outcomes. This may include surveys, interviews, and statistical analysis.

- Longitudinal Studies: Tracking the long-term impact of restorative justice on participants and communities is essential. This can help determine whether the benefits are sustained over time.

- Feedback and Participant Surveys: Gathering feedback from victims, offenders, and affected parties about their experiences and perceptions of the process.

- Comparative Analysis: Comparing the outcomes of restorative justice cases with those processed through traditional justice systems can provide insights into the effectiveness of restorative practices.

- Cultural Sensitivity: Ensuring that measurement tools are culturally sensitive and relevant to diverse communities is crucial for accurately capturing outcomes.

Overall, measuring outcomes in restorative justice is important for demonstrating its effectiveness, improving practices, and advocating for its continued growth as a valuable approach to addressing harm and promoting healing.

The lack of a legal framework for restorative practices can present several challenges:

1. Inconsistent Application: Without a clear legal framework, the application of restorative justice may be inconsistent. Different practitioners or jurisdictions may interpret and implement restorative practices in various ways, leading to inequities in access and outcomes.

2. Legitimacy and Trust: A well-established legal framework can enhance the legitimacy and trust in restorative justice processes. It provides a clear mandate for the use of

restorative practices, making them more acceptable to the public, victims, and offenders.

3. Standardization: A legal framework can standardize restorative justice practices, ensuring that they meet specific criteria and adhere to best practices. This consistency is essential for the effectiveness and reliability of restorative processes.

4. Procedural Safeguards: Legal frameworks often include procedural safeguards that protect the rights and interests of all parties involved. Without these safeguards, there may be concerns about due process and fairness.

5. Accountability: A legal framework provides a mechanism for holding practitioners and facilitators accountable for their actions. It sets out the expectations and responsibilities of those involved in restorative justice processes.

6. Enforceability: Legal support can make the outcomes of restorative justice processes more enforceable. Agreements reached through restorative practices may have legal weight, providing added incentives for compliance.

7. Public Funding: Legal recognition can facilitate the allocation of public funds to support restorative justice programs. This financial support is crucial for their sustainability and growth.

8. Victim and Offender Confidence: Victims and offenders may have greater confidence in the process when it operates within a legal framework. They may be more willing to participate if they know that their rights and interests are protected by law.

9. Consistent Ethical Standards: Legal frameworks often include ethical standards that practitioners must adhere to. These

standards help ensure that restorative justice processes are conducted ethically and responsibly.

To address the lack of a legal framework for restorative practices, efforts can be made to advocate for legislative support and the development of legal guidelines that provide a clear and consistent framework for the application of restorative justice. This may involve working with lawmakers, legal experts, and community stakeholders to create and implement legislation that supports the principles and practices of restorative justice while ensuring due process and fairness. Such efforts can enhance the effectiveness, legitimacy, and acceptance of restorative practices within the legal system.

CHAPTER 12

CONTEPOLARY RELEVANCE

Restorative justice plays a crucial role in the ongoing efforts for criminal justice reform. The contemporary criminal justice system faces a range of challenges, and restorative justice principles, inspired by the teachings of Romans, offer valuable alternatives and solutions to these issues:

1. Over-Incarceration: Restorative justice promotes a more balanced and proportional response to offenses. Instead of resorting to lengthy prison sentences for non-violent and low-level offenses, restorative justice offers a way to address harm and wrongdoing without the need for incarceration. This approach can help alleviate the problem of over-incarceration, which has strained prison systems and disproportionately affected certain communities.

2. Racial Disparities: Racial disparities in the criminal justice system are a deeply rooted problem. Restorative justice principles prioritize fairness, equity, and addressing the root causes of crime. By focusing on understanding and repairing harm,

restorative justice can help reduce racial disparities by addressing the underlying issues that lead to criminal behavior, rather than perpetuating systemic bias.

3. Recidivism: One of the central challenges in criminal justice is the high rate of recidivism, where individuals released from prison often reoffend. Restorative justice places a strong emphasis on accountability and addressing the underlying causes of criminal behavior. By involving offenders in the process of repairing harm and taking responsibility for their actions, restorative justice can contribute to reducing recidivism and promoting rehabilitation.

4. Healing and Reintegration: Traditional punitive justice systems often neglect the healing and reintegration of offenders into society. Restorative justice offers a holistic approach that recognizes the importance of addressing the harm caused to victims, helping offenders take responsibility for their actions, and facilitating their successful reintegration into the community. This approach not only benefits individuals but also contributes to safer and more cohesive communities.

5. Community Engagement: Restorative justice actively involves the community in the resolution of conflicts and the reintegration of offenders. This community engagement fosters a sense of ownership and responsibility for addressing crime and its consequences. It encourages collective efforts to create a more just and compassionate society.

In essence, restorative justice provides a promising avenue for addressing the pressing issues within the criminal justice system.

It shifts the focus from punitive measures to healing, accountability, and reintegration, aligning with the principles of fairness, compassion, and reconciliation inspired by the teachings of Romans. While it may not replace traditional criminal justice entirely, it offers a valuable and transformative complement that contributes to criminal justice reform efforts and paves the way for a more just and equitable system.

Community and social healing refer to the process of mending and revitalizing the relationships, trust, and cohesion within a community that may have been strained or damaged by conflicts, divisions, or various forms of harm. In today's interconnected world, communities often grapple with a range of challenges, including:

1. Conflicts: Communities may experience conflicts and disputes among individuals, groups, or institutions. These conflicts can lead to division, mistrust, and a breakdown of social bonds.

2. Prejudice and Discrimination: Prejudice and discrimination, whether based on race, ethnicity, religion, gender, or other factors, can lead to social divisions and exclusion. Addressing these issues is essential for building inclusive and equitable communities.

3. Social Divisions: Social divisions can arise from various factors, including economic disparities, political differences, and cultural diversity. These divisions can lead to fragmentation and hinder the well-being of the community as a whole.

In the context of community and social healing, the principles of reconciliation and restoration from Romans can play a pivotal role:

1. Reconciliation: Reconciliation involves bringing together individuals or groups who have been in conflict, helping them understand each other's perspectives, and finding common ground. Romans emphasizes the importance of reconciliation with God and among people, offering a model for addressing conflicts within communities.

2. Restoration: Restoration entails the repair and revitalization of relationships and trust within a community. Romans highlights the value of restoration in the context of personal transformation and healing, which can extend to the broader community.

3. Healing: Healing addresses the emotional, psychological, and social wounds caused by conflicts, divisions, and harm. The principles from Romans underscore the significance of healing and renewal, both at the individual and community levels.

4. Mending Social Rifts: The teachings of Romans can inform community-based initiatives that aim to mend social rifts. By emphasizing values of forgiveness, empathy, and understanding, these initiatives can create a sense of unity, shared purpose, and social cohesion within the community.

Community and social healing are vital for fostering resilient and harmonious communities. By drawing inspiration from the principles of reconciliation and restoration found in Romans, communities can work towards resolving conflicts, addressing prejudice, and bridging social divisions, ultimately building more inclusive and compassionate societies where individuals and groups coexist in harmony.

Conflict resolution and peacebuilding are essential processes aimed at resolving conflicts and promoting peace, both at local and global levels. In an increasingly interconnected world, various conflicts, whether they are local disputes or international tensions, demand effective approaches to de-escalate and address these issues. Restorative justice, inspired by the principles of Romans, offers a valuable framework for these processes by emphasizing dialogue, understanding, and reconciliation:

1. Conflict Resolution: Restorative justice, rooted in principles of accountability and reconciliation, provides a structured approach to addressing conflicts. It encourages all parties involved to engage in dialogue, understand the root causes of the conflict, and work together to find mutually agreeable solutions. This process can be applied to interpersonal disputes, community conflicts, and even larger-scale conflicts, helping to prevent escalation and fostering resolution.

2. Dialogue and Understanding: Central to restorative justice is the concept of open and meaningful dialogue. This dialogue creates an environment where all parties have the opportunity to express their perspectives and concerns. Through this process, individuals can develop a deeper understanding of the motivations and needs of others involved in the conflict. Romans' teachings on reconciliation and forgiveness align with the aim of promoting empathy and understanding, crucial elements in any conflict resolution process.

3. Reconciliation: Restorative justice places a strong emphasis on reconciliation, which is the process of repairing and restoring relationships that may have been damaged by the conflict. Romans highlights the importance of reconciling with one another, emphasizing forgiveness and healing. This concept is integral to peacebuilding efforts, as it fosters the re-establishment of trust and cooperation among parties in conflict.

4. Conflict Prevention: While often applied after a conflict has occurred, restorative justice principles can also contribute to conflict prevention. By addressing the underlying causes of conflicts and promoting understanding, individuals and communities can work proactively to reduce tensions and prevent conflicts from escalating.

5. Peacebuilding: Peacebuilding is a long-term process that aims to establish and maintain peace in the aftermath of conflicts. Restorative justice, inspired by Romans, aligns with this goal by focusing on repairing harm, promoting accountability, and fostering positive relationships. It contributes to sustainable peace by addressing the root causes of conflict.

6. International Diplomacy: Restorative justice principles can be applied at international levels through diplomacy and peace negotiations. The principles of accountability, dialogue, and reconciliation offer valuable tools for resolving international conflicts, bridging divides, and promoting lasting peace.

In summary, restorative justice, inspired by the teachings of Romans, provides a framework for conflict resolution and peacebuilding that emphasizes dialogue, understanding, and reconciliation. This approach is valuable not only in addressing conflicts but also in preventing them and contributing to lasting peace within communities and on a global scale.

Truth and reconciliation are integral components of transitional justice in post-conflict societies. Restorative justice principles, rooted in accountability and reconciliation, align closely with the goals of truth and reconciliation commissions. Here's how they intersect:

1. Uncovering Past Wrongs: Truth and reconciliation commissions aim to uncover and document past wrongs, including human rights abuses and crimes committed during conflicts or oppressive regimes. These commissions create a platform for victims and perpetrators to share their experiences and for society to confront its history. Restorative justice principles emphasize acknowledging wrongdoing and the need for truth as a foundation for accountability.

2. Accountability: Restorative justice underscores the importance of holding individuals accountable for their actions. Truth and reconciliation commissions serve a similar purpose by identifying those responsible for human rights violations and ensuring they face appropriate consequences, whether through legal proceedings or alternative forms of accountability. Restorative justice processes within these commissions can include acknowledgment of wrongdoing and sincere expressions of remorse.

3. Victim-Centered Approaches: Restorative justice places victims at the center of the process, ensuring their voices are heard and their needs are addressed. Truth and reconciliation

commissions similarly prioritize the experiences and needs of victims, providing a space for them to share their stories and seek acknowledgment and reparations.

4. Healing and Reconciliation: Restorative justice seeks to promote healing and reconciliation, not only between individuals but within communities and society at large. Truth and reconciliation commissions aim to facilitate national healing by acknowledging past wrongs, fostering understanding, and promoting reconciliation. Both approaches recognize the significance of addressing the emotional and psychological wounds left by conflicts.

5. Preventing Recurrence: Both restorative justice and truth and reconciliation commissions aim to prevent the recurrence of violence and injustice. They do so by addressing the root causes of conflict, exposing the consequences of past wrongdoing, and establishing a framework for building a just and peaceful society.

6. Public Acknowledgment: Restorative justice emphasizes the public acknowledgment of wrongdoing, and truth and reconciliation commissions provide a forum for this acknowledgment on a national scale. This acknowledgment is critical for both individual and societal healing and for breaking the cycle of denial and impunity.

In summary, truth and reconciliation commissions and restorative justice principles share a common objective in addressing the legacy of violence and injustice in post-conflict societies. They aim to uncover past wrongs, foster accountability, promote healing, and prevent the recurrence of conflict. The principles of acknowledgment, accountability, and reconciliation are central to both approaches, making them complementary in transitional justice processes.

Restorative practices in schools, while highly beneficial, are not as common as they should be for several reasons. These practices, inspired by principles found in Romans, can play a significant role in addressing bullying and school violence, as well as in creating a safe and inclusive learning environment. Here are some factors contributing to their limited implementation:

1. Lack of Awareness: Many educators and school administrators may not be fully aware of restorative practices and their potential benefits. Awareness and education are crucial to encouraging the adoption of these practices in schools.

2. Traditional Disciplinary Approaches: The traditional punitive approach to discipline, such as suspensions and expulsions, has been the norm in many schools. Transitioning to restorative practices requires a shift in mindset and a willingness to explore alternative methods of addressing behavioral issues.

3. Resistance to Change: Resistance to change is a common barrier in many institutions, including schools. Implementing restorative practices may face opposition from those who are comfortable with the status quo or are hesitant to try new approaches.

4. Training and Resources: Effective implementation of restorative practices requires proper training and resources for educators and school staff. Many schools may lack the resources and funding needed to provide this training.

5. Measuring Outcomes: Some school systems focus on quantifiable outcomes, such as standardized test scores, and may be hesitant to invest in restorative practices that have less easily measurable outcomes, even though the long-term benefits are significant.

6. Complexity of Implementation: Restorative practices involve complex interpersonal dynamics and require a deep understanding of the principle involved. This complexity can deter some schools from adopting these practices.

7. Time and Commitment: Restorative practices demand time and commitment from both educators and students. Some may be concerned about the time investment needed, as well as whether students will be receptive to the process.

Despite these challenges, restorative practices hold great promise in addressing bullying and school violence. These practices encourage dialogue, empathy, and accountability, creating an environment where students feel a sense of belonging and are more likely to address and resolve conflicts in a constructive way. By promoting the principles of Romans – acknowledgment, responsibility, and reconciliation – restorative practices have the potential to create safer and more inclusive learning environments in schools, making them a valuable investment in the well-being of students and the overall school community.

Victims of crime indeed require comprehensive support to navigate the physical, emotional, and psychological impact of their experiences. Modern victim support services can greatly benefit from integrating restorative justice principles to empower victims, address their needs, and facilitate their healing journey. Here's how restorative justice can enhance victim support:

1. Empowerment: Restorative justice principles emphasize the empowerment of victims, giving them a voice and a role in the process. Victim support services can integrate these principles by providing victims with opportunities to express their feelings, needs, and preferences. Empowering victims in this way helps them regain a sense of control over their lives and their recovery.

2. Acknowledgment and Validation: Restorative justice encourages the acknowledgment of the harm done to victims. Support services can use this principle to validate victims' experiences and provide a safe space for them to share their stories. This acknowledgment can be a crucial step in the healing process.

3. Individualized Support: Victim support services can adopt an individualized approach to meet each victim's unique needs. Restorative justice principles promote tailoring the response to the specific circumstances of each case, which aligns with providing personalized support to victims.

4. Healing-Centered Approaches: Restorative justice focuses on healing and reconciliation, not only for offenders but also for victims. Victim support services can incorporate these healing-centered approaches by offering counseling, therapy, and resources that promote emotional and psychological recovery.

5. Restitution and Compensation: Restorative justice principles include the concept of restitution and making amends. Victim support services can help victims access compensation, financial support, or restitution when applicable, ensuring they receive fair and just reparations for their losses.

6. Restorative Justice Programs: Some victim support services are involved in restorative justice programs, where victims have the option to participate in processes that involve dialogue with offenders. These programs allow victims to ask questions, seek answers, and find closure, contributing to their emotional recovery.

7. Education and Awareness: Victim support services can educate victims about restorative justice principles and processes, allowing them to make informed decisions about their involvement in legal proceedings and restorative justice practices.

8. Long-Term Support: Restorative justice principles recognize that the impact of harm can be long-lasting. Victim support services should also provide long-term support, as needed, to help victims as they continue on their healing journey.

Incorporating restorative justice principles into victim support services can significantly enhance the quality of care and assistance provided to victims. By empowering victims, acknowledging their experiences, and promoting healing, these services can better address the complex and multifaceted needs of victims of crime, ultimately contributing to their recovery and well-being.

The global relevance of the teachings of Romans on restorative justice is evident in their adaptability to diverse regions and cultures. Here are examples from various parts of the world where these principles have been embraced to address local and global challenges:

1. South Africa: The Truth and Reconciliation Commission in South Africa, chaired by Archbishop Desmond Tutu, employed

restorative justice principles to address the legacy of apartheid. It allowed victims and perpetrators to come forward, acknowledge wrongdoings, and work towards reconciliation. This approach served as a model for post-conflict societies worldwide.

2. Canada: Canada's Indigenous communities have been applying restorative justice principles in their justice systems. These principles are incorporated into the sentencing of offenders, emphasizing community involvement and the restoration of harmony.

3. Scandinavian Countries: Countries like Norway and Sweden have implemented restorative justice practices in their criminal justice systems. They focus on rehabilitation and reintegration rather than punitive measures, resulting in lower recidivism rates and safer communities.

4. Middle East: Organizations like the Sulha Peace Project in the Middle East use restorative justice principles to promote dialogue and reconciliation in conflict-ridden areas. They facilitate encounters between people of different backgrounds and encourage communication to build bridges.

5. Australia: Restorative justice practices are widely used in Australian schools to address issues like bullying and student conflicts. These practices create a more inclusive and respectful learning environment.

6. Restorative Circles in Brazil: Favelas in Brazil have seen the implementation of restorative circles, a community-based approach to resolving conflicts and promoting social cohesion. These circles have helped reduce violence and improve community relations.

7. The Balkans: The Balkans region, which experienced violent conflicts in the 1990s, has seen initiatives that draw from restorative justice principles to promote reconciliation and healing among different ethnic groups.

8. United States: Restorative justice programs have been introduced in various U.S. states, particularly within the juvenile justice system. These programs aim to divert young offenders from the traditional justice system and provide opportunities for rehabilitation.

9. International Tribunals: International criminal tribunals, such as the International Criminal Court (ICC), draw on restorative justice principles when determining sentences for individuals found guilty of war crimes, crimes against humanity, and genocide.

10. Community-Based Initiatives: Grassroots community organizations worldwide have adopted restorative justice practices to address local disputes, build trust, and promote reconciliation.

The global adoption of restorative justice principles, inspired by the teachings of Romans, reflects their adaptability and effectiveness in addressing a wide range of challenges, from post-conflict reconciliation to school bullying. These principles provide a framework for dialogue, acknowledgment, accountability, healing, and the promotion of a just and inclusive society, making them relevant and applicable on a global scale.

Interfaith and interdisciplinary dialogues are indeed crucial when it comes to leveraging the teachings of Romans on restorative justice. Here's why these dialogues are important:

1. Diversity of Perspectives: Interfaith dialogues bring together representatives from different faith traditions, fostering a rich exchange of perspectives on restorative justice. This diversity helps in creating a more comprehensive and inclusive understanding of how these principles can be applied.

2. Shared Values: Many faith traditions share common values related to justice, forgiveness, and reconciliation. By engaging in interfaith dialogues, practitioners and scholars can identify these shared values and work towards a collective understanding of restorative justice.

3. Interdisciplinary Collaboration: Restorative justice is inherently interdisciplinary, drawing from fields like law, psychology, sociology, and theology. Interdisciplinary dialogues enable experts from various disciplines to collaborate and develop a holistic approach to restorative justice that considers multiple dimensions.

4. Conflict Resolution: Restorative justice is often applied in conflict resolution contexts. Interfaith and interdisciplinary dialogues can provide insights and strategies for applying these principles to manage conflicts effectively and promote peace.

5. Global Perspectives: Restorative justice has global relevance, and international perspectives are valuable. Engaging in interfaith and interdisciplinary dialogues with a global focus allows for the exchange of practices, lessons, and innovations from various parts of the world.

6. Ethical Considerations: Restorative justice is deeply rooted in ethical considerations. Interfaith dialogues can contribute

to ethical discussions, helping to define common ethical principles that underpin restorative justice practices.

7. Education and Advocacy: Interfaith and interdisciplinary dialogues can play a role in educating communities and advocating for the adoption of restorative justice principles in various settings, including schools, criminal justice systems, and conflict resolution programs.

8. Practical Applications: By bringing together individuals from diverse backgrounds and disciplines, these dialogues can result in practical strategies and guidelines for implementing restorative justice in real-world situations.

9. Overcoming Misconceptions: Restorative justice may have misconceptions or biases associated with it. Interfaith and interdisciplinary dialogues can help dispel these misconceptions and foster a more accurate and informed understanding of the approach.

10. Community Building: These dialogues can promote community building and strengthen the bonds between faith communities, academics, practitioners, and policymakers, all of whom play a role in advancing restorative justice.

In essence, interfaith and interdisciplinary dialogues not only enrich the understanding of restorative justice but also offer a platform for collaboration, advocacy, and the development of practical applications. They provide a space where shared values, ethical considerations, and diverse perspectives converge to advance the cause of justice, healing, and reconciliation, as inspired by the teachings of Romans and embraced by a global and diverse community.

CHAPTER 13

RESTORATIVE JUSTICE IN THE CHURCH

Restorative justice in the church refers to the application of restorative principles within the Christian community. It involves understanding, embracing, and practicing restorative justice principles as inspired by the teachings of Jesus Christ and the theological foundations found in the Bible, particularly in the Book of Romans. This approach emphasizes healing, reconciliation, and accountability and aligns with core Christian values of love, forgiveness, and grace.

In the church context, restorative justice involves:

1. Biblical Foundation: Restorative justice in the church is firmly grounded in the Bible, especially in the teachings of the Apostle Paul in the Book of Romans. It draws from these theological underpinnings to shape the church's approach to addressing harm and conflict.

2. Congregational Engagement: The church community actively engages with restorative justice principles. This encompasses not only understanding and discussing these principles but putting them into practice within the church's internal affairs.

3. Conflict Resolution: Restorative justice in the church provides a framework for resolving conflicts, promoting healing, and maintaining unity among church members. It encourages open communication, understanding, and reconciliation.

4. Ministry and Outreach: The church extends its involvement in restorative justice beyond its own walls. It plays a role in addressing broader societal issues, such as supporting those affected by crime, advocating for criminal justice reform, and promoting healing and reconciliation in the community.

5. Victim Support: The church offers support and care for victims, acknowledging their suffering, and helping them on their journey to healing. It prioritizes the restoration of dignity for those who have been harmed.

6. Promoting Reconciliation: Restorative justice in the church places a strong emphasis on the power of reconciliation, both within the church community and in the wider world. It encourages the restoration of broken relationships and the building of bridges between individuals and communities.

7. Moral Leadership: The church serves as a moral leader, advocating for restorative justice principles in the criminal justice system. It speaks out against punitive measures and promotes a vision of justice that emphasizes rehabilitation, reconciliation, and healing.

In essence, restorative justice in the church reflects the application of Christian values and theological principles to address harm, resolve conflicts, and promote healing and reconciliation. It recognizes the church as a powerful force for transformation and justice within the Christian community and the broader society.

The biblical foundation of restorative justice in the Book of Romans is deeply rooted in the teachings of the Apostle Paul and the theological principles he expounds in this epistle. These teachings provide a strong biblical basis for restorative justice principles. Here's how the Book of Romans forms the foundation:

1. Reconciliation: The central theme of reconciliation runs throughout the Book of Romans. In Romans 5:10 (NIV), Paul writes, "For if, while we were God's enemies, we were reconciled to him through the death of his Son, how much more, having been reconciled, shall we be saved through his life!" This verse underscores the idea of reconciliation, which is fundamental in restorative justice. It emphasizes the restoration of relationships and the healing of divisions.

2. Forgiveness: Romans also addresses the concept of forgiveness. In Romans 12:19-21 (NIV), Paul exhorts, "Do not take revenge, my dear friends, but leave room for God's wrath, for it is written: 'It is mine to avenge; I will repay,' says the Lord. On the contrary: 'If your enemy is hungry, feed him; if he is thirsty, give him something to drink. In doing this, you will hear burning coals on his head.'" This passage highlights the Christian value of forgiveness, a core principle in restorative justice.

3. Love and Compassion: Love and compassion are central to restorative justice. Romans 13:10 (NIV) states, "Love does no harm to a neighbor. Therefore, love is the fulfillment of the law." This verse emphasizes the importance of love and non-harm, which are foundational principles in restorative justice practices.

4. Accountability: Romans teaches the concept of accountability. In Romans 14:12 (NIV), it says, "So then, each of us will give an account of ourselves to God." This verse highlights personal accountability, a crucial element in the restorative justice process.

5. Transformation: Romans speaks of personal transformation and renewal through faith in Christ. Romans 12:2 (NIV) states, "Do not conform to the pattern of this world but be transformed by the renewing of your mind." Transformation is a key aspect of restorative justice, as it signifies a commitment to change one's behavior and contribute positively to society.

6. Justice and Mercy: The Book of Romans grapples with the balance between justice and mercy, reflecting the tension often present in restorative justice practices. Romans 9:15 (NIV) addresses the concept of God's mercy, "I will have mercy on whom I have mercy, and I will have compassion on whom I have compassion." Restorative justice seeks to harmonize justice and mercy, just as the Book of Romans does.

The Book of Romans, with its emphasis on reconciliation, forgiveness, love, accountability, transformation, and the interplay of justice and mercy, provides a robust biblical foundation for restorative justice principles. These teachings align with core Christian values and offer guidance on how individuals and communities can address harm, promote healing, and restore relationships in accordance with their faith.

Congregational engagement in the practices of restorative justice within the Christian church can have a profoundly positive impact. Here are several ways in which this engagement can influence and enhance restorative justice practices:

1. Promoting Understanding: Congregational engagement involves educating and involving the church community in understanding the principles of restorative justice. This can include sermons, study groups, and workshops that help members grasp the theological and practical aspects of restorative justice. A well-informed congregation is better equipped to support and implement these principles.

2. Creating a Supportive Environment: The church community can become a safe and supportive environment for those affected by harm or conflict. Congregational members can offer emotional and spiritual support to victims and offenders, recognizing the importance of healing and reconciliation.

3. Conflict Resolution: The church can actively use restorative justice principles to address conflicts and disagreements within the congregation. This approach fosters open dialogue, understanding, and reconciliation, preventing issues from escalating and creating division.

4. Accountability: The church can model accountability by holding individuals responsible for their actions. This is vital in demonstrating the principles of restorative justice, as it emphasizes personal responsibility and the consequences of one's behavior.

5. Reconciliation: The congregation can actively promote reconciliation and restoration of relationships, not only within the church but also in the broader community. The church can serve as a beacon of hope, showing that forgiveness, healing, and unity are possible.

6. Ministry and Outreach: Engaging in restorative justice practices means extending support to those beyond the church community. This may involve advocating for criminal justice reform, supporting victims of crime, and offering healing and reconciliation to the broader society.

7. Moral Leadership: The church, through its leaders and members, can provide moral leadership in advocating for restorative justice principles in the broader society. It can be a strong voice for alternatives to punitive justice systems, emphasizing rehabilitation and reconciliation.

8. Victim Support: The congregation can actively engage in supporting victims, acknowledging their suffering, and helping them on their journey to healing. This support is essential in restoring the dignity of those who have been harmed.

9. Teaching and Modeling Love and Forgiveness: The church community can teach and model Christian values of love and forgiveness, which are core principles of restorative justice. Congregational members can exemplify these values in their interactions with one another and the broader community.

10. Promoting Transformation: Encouraging personal transformation is a vital part of restorative justice. The congregation can provide an environment that supports individuals in their commitment to change, contributing positively to society.

Congregational engagement positively affects the practices of restorative justice by creating a well-informed, supportive, and accountable community that actively promotes understanding, reconciliation, and the application of Christian values. The church can serve as a living example of the restorative justice principles found in the teachings of the Apostle Paul in the Book of Romans, inspiring individuals to seek healing, forgiveness, and reconciliation.

Conflict resolution within the church is a vital aspect of maintaining unity and harmony among its members. Restorative justice principles, inspired by the teachings of Romans, can offer effective tools for addressing conflicts and promoting healing within the church community. Here's how conflict resolution can align with these principles:

1. Open Dialogue: Restorative justice encourages open and honest dialogue. In conflicts within the church, this means providing a safe space for those involved to express their concerns, perspectives, and emotions. Encouraging open communication is in line with the principle of addressing harm and understanding one another.

2. Understanding the Impact: Restorative justice asks individuals to consider the impact of their actions on others. In conflict resolution, this means helping parties involved in the dispute to understand how their words or actions have affected others. It fosters empathy and compassion, which are essential for healing and reconciliation.

3. Accountability: Restorative justice emphasizes personal responsibility. In the context of church conflict resolution, this means encouraging those involved to take responsibility for their words or actions that contributed to the dispute. Acknowledging one's role in the conflict is a crucial step in the restoration process.

4. Making Amends: Just as making amends is central to restorative justice, it's essential in resolving church conflicts. Parties involved can work together to find ways to repair the harm caused. This may involve apologies, acts of service, or other gestures of reconciliation.

5. Reconciliation: Restorative justice seeks reconciliation as its ultimate goal. In church conflict resolution, the focus should be on rebuilding relationships and promoting unity. Encouraging forgiveness and seeking reconciliation align with the principles found in the Book of Romans.

6. Community Involvement: Restorative justice often involves the wider community in the resolution process. In the context of church conflicts, this can mean seeking advice or mediation from church leaders, elders, or congregation members who can support the resolution efforts.

7. Restoring Dignity: The church should always seek to restore the dignity of those involved in the conflict. Treating each party with respect and acknowledging their worth as individuals created in God's image is essential for the healing process.

8. Transformation and Renewal: Restorative justice encourages personal transformation. In the church, this transformation may involve a change in behavior, attitudes, or

perspectives, allowing individuals to contribute positively to the community and prevent future conflicts.

9. Forgiveness and Repentance: Encouraging forgiveness and repentance is integral to resolving conflicts in the church. Embracing these principles aligns with the Christian values of love, grace, and reconciliation found in Romans.

By applying these restorative justice principles, church leaders and members can effectively resolve conflicts, promote healing, and maintain unity within the church community. These principles offer a pathway to address disputes in a way that reflects the teachings of the Apostle Paul in Romans, fostering a culture of understanding, forgiveness, and reconciliation.

Ministry and outreach in the context of the Book of Romans and restorative justice encompass a broad and impactful approach to addressing societal issues. Here are some ways in which churches can engage in ministry and outreach inspired by restorative justice principles:

1. Supporting Victims: Churches can provide vital support for individuals who have been victims of crime. This can include counseling, emotional support, and practical assistance. Restorative justice encourages empathy and care for those who have suffered harm, aligning with the Christian values of compassion and love.

2. Advocating for Criminal Justice Reform: Restorative justice principles emphasize a shift from punitive to restorative measures. Churches can engage in advocacy efforts for criminal justice reform, pushing for policies that emphasize rehabilitation, reintegration, and addressing the root causes of crime.

3. Reentry Programs: Supporting individuals reintegrating into society after serving time in the criminal justice system is crucial. Churches can establish reentry programs that provide resources, mentorship, and a supportive community for those looking to rebuild their lives. This aligns with restorative justice's emphasis on transformation and renewal.

4. Community Building: Restorative justice is about repairing harm and building stronger, more harmonious communities. Churches can engage in community-building initiatives, fostering relationships, trust, and unity among their members and the broader community.

5. Restorative Practices: Churches can incorporate restorative practices within their own community, using restorative circles or mediation to address conflicts and promote healing. These practices can be extended to the community at large, helping resolve disputes and foster reconciliation.

6. Restorative Justice Education: Educating the congregation and the community about restorative justice principles, their biblical foundations, and their practical applications can empower individuals to engage in these practices in their own lives and support them in wider society.

7. Social Justice Initiatives: Addressing societal injustices is a fundamental aspect of restorative justice. Churches can initiate and support social justice campaigns that tackle issues such as poverty, inequality, racism, and discrimination. These efforts align with the principles of addressing harm and promoting equity.

8. Prison Ministry: Engaging in prison ministry provides spiritual and emotional support to incarcerated individuals. It can

also be a platform for sharing restorative justice principles, offering hope for personal transformation and redemption.

9. Victim-Offender Dialogue: Encouraging victim-offender dialogue and reconciliation processes can be part of the outreach efforts. These dialogues can help both victims and offenders find closure and healing, in line with restorative justice goals.

10. Refugee and Migrant Support: Churches can actively support refugees and migrants, helping them find shelter, resources, and community. Restorative justice principles emphasize empathy and hospitality, which align with the support needed by those forced to leave their homes.

In summary, ministry and outreach in the context of the Book of Romans and restorative justice entail a comprehensive and compassionate approach to addressing societal issues. It involves supporting victims, advocating for reform, providing reentry programs, building community, practicing restorative approaches, and actively engaging with social justice initiatives. Through these actions, churches can extend the principles of restorative justice to create a more just, compassionate, and reconciled society.

Victim support is imperative for several significant reasons, and the church plays a vital role in this crucial aspect of restorative justice:

1. Compassion and Empathy: One of the core principles of restorative justice is empathy and compassion for those who have suffered harm. The church, rooted in Christian teachings, exemplifies these values by extending care and support to victims.

This not only aligns with Christian values but also with the restorative justice goal of acknowledging the pain of victims.

2. Healing and Restoration: Victims often go through a traumatic experience that can leave lasting emotional and psychological scars. The church can provide a safe space for victims to heal, seek counseling, and find comfort in their faith. This healing process is essential for restoring victims' well-being, in line with restorative justice's focus on repairing harm.

3. Dignity and Worth: Restorative justice places a strong emphasis on recognizing the inherent dignity and worth of every individual. Supporting victims in their journey to recovery and justice restoration is a practical way to affirm their dignity. The church's role in this process aligns with the Christian belief in the sanctity of human life.

4. Rebuilding Trust: Victims may often feel a loss of trust in their community and the world at large. The church, through its support, can contribute to rebuilding trust in others, as well as trust in the possibility of healing and restoration. This restoration of trust is a fundamental aspect of restorative justice.

5. Community and Belonging: The church serves as a community of faith and belonging. By providing support for victims, it reinforces the idea that victims are not alone in their suffering. Restorative justice seeks to repair the social bonds that are strained by harm, and the church plays a key role in reestablishing a sense of community.

6. Moral and Ethical Responsibility: For the church, extending support to victims is a moral and ethical responsibility. It reflects the Christian commitment to love, compassion, and helping

those in need. This sense of responsibility resonates with the restorative justice principle of addressing the needs of those who have been harmed.

7. Promoting Forgiveness and Reconciliation: Restorative justice encourages processes of forgiveness and reconciliation. While these are personal journeys, the church can offer guidance and a spiritual foundation for individuals seeking to forgive or reconcile with those who have caused harm.

8. Advocacy for Victims: The church can also play a role in advocating for the rights and needs of victims within the wider community and even in the criminal justice system. This advocacy is in alignment with the restorative justice principle of ensuring that victims have a voice in the process.

In conclusion, victim support is imperative for its role in healing, restoring dignity, and rebuilding trust for those who have experienced harm. The church, driven by its Christian values, has a unique responsibility in this regard and plays a crucial part in implementing restorative justice principles. By providing support and care to victims, the church contributes to a more compassionate and just society.

Promoting reconciliation within the Christian community involves the active participation of various individuals and groups. Here are key stakeholders involved in fostering reconciliation:

1. Church Leaders: Church leaders, including pastors, priests, and elders, play a pivotal role in promoting reconciliation. They can provide guidance, counsel, and pastoral care to

individuals and families in conflict. Their leadership can set the tone for the entire congregation.

2. Church Members: The congregation itself is a significant part of the reconciliation process. Church members can support one another in times of conflict, offer forgiveness, and extend a helping hand to those in need. The church community is ideally positioned to model reconciliation for the broader society.

3. Counselors and Mediators: Trained counselors and mediators can be valuable resources within the church. They can facilitate communication, help resolve disputes, and guide individuals and families toward reconciliation. Their expertise is especially important when conflicts involve complex dynamics.

4. Families: The church places a strong emphasis on the importance of family. Families are often at the heart of conflicts, and their involvement is essential for reconciliation. Parents, children, and extended family members can work together to heal relational wounds and restore harmony.

5. Small Groups and Support Networks: Many churches organize small groups and support networks. These settings provide opportunities for individuals to share their struggles, receive emotional support, and explore ways to reconcile with one another.

6. Community Engagement: Reconciliation isn't limited to internal church matters. Churches can engage with the broader community to promote reconciliation in society at large. This can involve outreach programs, community service, and advocacy for peace and reconciliation.

7. Prayer and Spiritual Guidance: Prayer and spiritual guidance are central to the Christian approach to reconciliation. The

church community can come together in prayer to seek God's guidance and strength in the process of reconciliation.

8. Restorative Justice Ministries: Some churches have specialized ministries or teams dedicated to restorative justice. These groups are focused on addressing conflicts, promoting healing, and actively practicing restorative justice principles within the church and in the community.

9. Youth and Children: Younger members of the church play a significant role in fostering reconciliation. Youth groups and children's ministries can instill values of forgiveness, empathy, and conflict resolution from an early age, contributing to a culture of reconciliation in the future.

10. Outreach to the Marginalized: The church can engage in outreach to marginalized and vulnerable individuals and communities, offering reconciliation and healing to those who have been excluded or harmed by society.

11. Reconciliation Services: Some churches hold specific reconciliation services or events, where individuals are encouraged to come forward and seek forgiveness or reconciliation with others. These services can be powerful catalysts for healing and unity.

12. Education and Awareness: Churches can educate their members about the importance of reconciliation, forgiveness, and restorative justice. By raising awareness, they empower individuals to actively pursue reconciliation in their lives.

In conclusion, promoting reconciliation within the Christian community involves the collective efforts of church leaders, members, counselors, families, small groups, and the wider community. It's a collaborative endeavor guided by Christian principles of forgiveness, healing, and restoration.

Moral leadership in the context of restorative justice within the church involves the church community and its leaders taking a principled and ethical stand in advocating for restorative practices in the criminal justice system. Here are key aspects of moral leadership in this context:

1. Advocating for Compassion: Moral leaders within the church promote compassion as a central value in the criminal justice system. They emphasize the need to view offenders as individuals in need of healing and restoration, rather than solely as wrongdoers deserving punishment.

2. Rehabilitation Over Retribution: Moral leadership encourages a shift from retribution-focused approaches to rehabilitation-focused ones. Leaders advocate for policies and practices that prioritize the rehabilitation of offenders, aiming to address the root causes of their actions and prevent future harm.

3. Supporting Victim-Centered Approaches: Moral leaders acknowledge the importance of supporting victims of crime and advocating for their needs. They work to ensure that restorative justice practices prioritize the healing and well-being of victims, allowing them to participate in the process and have their voices heard.

4. Promoting Reconciliation: The church's moral leadership emphasizes the transformative power of reconciliation. Leaders encourage criminal justice systems to incorporate restorative justice principles that facilitate dialogue, forgiveness, and the rebuilding of trust between offenders and victims.

5. Healing and Restoration: Moral leaders advocate for the inclusion of healing and restoration as core components of the criminal justice process. They recognize that true justice involves not only addressing the harm caused by offenses but also helping individuals rebuild their lives in a positive and productive manner.

6. Addressing Systemic Injustices: Church leaders, as moral advocates, address systemic injustices within the criminal justice system. They work to eliminate disparities and biases that disproportionately affect marginalized and vulnerable populations.

7. Educational Initiatives: Moral leaders within the church take an active role in educating their congregations and the broader community about the principles of restorative justice. They raise awareness of the potential for transformation and healing through these practices.

8. Prayer and Spiritual Guidance: Moral leaders engage in prayer and spiritual guidance to seek wisdom and guidance in their advocacy for restorative justice. They encourage their congregations to pray for both victims and offenders, emphasizing the importance of spiritual support in the healing process.

9. Community Engagement: Moral leadership extends beyond the walls of the church. Church leaders engage with the broader community, law enforcement agencies, policymakers, and advocacy groups to promote restorative justice principles and advocate for criminal justice reform.

10. Policy and Legislative Advocacy: Moral leaders may engage in policy and legislative advocacy to bring about changes in

the criminal justice system. They work with lawmakers to develop and support legislation that aligns with restorative justice principles.

11. Nonviolent Resistance: Moral leaders may advocate for nonviolent resistance to oppressive or punitive measures within the criminal justice system. This can include peaceful protests, civil disobedience, and public awareness campaigns.

In summary, moral leadership within the church involves advocating for a compassionate, healing-oriented, and reconciliatory approach to criminal justice. It is rooted in the principles of love, forgiveness, and the pursuit of justice as seen in the teachings of Jesus Christ, as well as in the teachings of Romans on restorative justice.

Case Studies:

Case studies are real-life examples or stories that illustrate the practical application of restorative justice principles within the Christian community. They are essential for several reasons:

1. Concrete Illustration: Case studies provide concrete and tangible examples of how restorative justice is put into practice. They give readers a clear understanding of how the principles discussed in theory are applied in real-life situations.

2. Inspiration: Case studies can inspire individuals, churches, and communities to adopt restorative justice practices. When people see successful examples and positive outcomes, they are more likely to become motivated to implement similar approaches.

3. Learning Opportunities: By examining case studies, readers can learn from both the successes and challenges faced by others. They can gain insights into what works well and what

pitfalls to avoid when implementing restorative justice within a Christian context.

4. Contextual Relevance: Case studies can be tailored to specific contexts, allowing readers to relate to situations and challenges that are similar to their own. This contextual relevance makes the application of restorative justice more relatable and achievable.

5. Testimonials of Transformation: Case studies often highlight stories of personal transformation, redemption, and reconciliation. These stories emphasize the positive impact of restorative justice and demonstrate that individuals can change and make amends.

6. Demonstration of Christian Values: Case studies can showcase how restorative justice aligns with Christian values of love, forgiveness, and reconciliation. They demonstrate how the principles derived from the teachings of Romans can be put into action.

7. Building Support: Sharing successful case studies can help build support for restorative justice initiatives within the church and the broader community. They serve as evidence of the effectiveness of these practices.

8. Challenge Stereotypes: Case studies can challenge stereotypes and preconceptions about offenders and victims. They humanize the individuals involved and show that everyone has the potential for healing and transformation.

9. Promoting Accountability: Case studies often highlight the importance of accountability and making amends, emphasizing that justice can be achieved through actions that repair harm.

10. Fostering Dialogue: These real-life stories can foster dialogue and discussion within the church community, encouraging members to consider the practical application of restorative justice principles in their own lives.

In the context of restorative justice in the church, case studies serve as powerful tools for both education and advocacy. They demonstrate that restorative justice is not just a theoretical concept but a practical and effective approach that can lead to healing, reconciliation, and transformation within the Christian community.

CHAPTER 14

BUILDING A RESTORATIVE SOCIETY

Building a Restorative Society is of paramount importance in our lives for several compelling reasons:

Restorative justice offers a path to healing for individuals and communities affected by harm and conflict. It allows for open dialogue, empathy, and the possibility of forgiveness, facilitating the process of reconciliation and emotional recovery.

In a restorative society, individuals are held accountable for their actions while also being provided opportunities for personal growth and positive change. This approach is crucial for preventing repeat offenses and supporting rehabilitation.

Embracing restorative justice in the criminal justice system can significantly reduce recidivism rates. When offenders are actively engaged in making amends and understanding the impact of their actions, they are less likely to reoffend.

Restorative justice practices foster a sense of community. By involving community members in addressing harm and conflict, it strengthens social bonds and promotes a collective responsibility for maintaining a safe and harmonious environment.

Implementing restorative justice principles in schools creates a positive and inclusive learning environment. It addresses issues like bullying and conflict resolution, ultimately leading to better academic and social outcomes for students.

In a world marked by divisions and conflicts, restorative justice can heal rifts, promote understanding, and contribute to unity within communities. It offers a space for dialogue and resolution, even in deeply divided societies.

Restorative justice can address historical injustices and promote healing on a national level. Truth and reconciliation commissions, guided by restorative principles, allow societies to come to terms with their past and move forward with unity.

Restorative justice principles empower marginalized communities by addressing systemic inequalities and promoting social justice. This empowers individuals to advocate for their rights and dismantles oppressive structures.

Restorative justice transcends religious and ideological boundaries. Interfaith and interdisciplinary dialogues can leverage these principles to promote shared values of justice, healing, and reconciliation.

The global acceptance of restorative justice exemplifies its universal relevance. Examples from around the world show how these principles can address a wide range of local and global challenges.

The vision of a restorative society serves as a call to action, inspiring individuals to work towards a world where restorative justice is not just an option but a way of life. It emphasizes the ongoing effort required to create a more compassionate, accountable, and reconciled world.

Incorporating restorative justice principles in our lives and society can lead to profound positive changes, promoting healing, accountability, and unity. It empowers individuals to take an active role in resolving conflicts and addressing harm, ultimately contributing to a more just and harmonious world.

Restorative justice in the criminal justice system is of paramount importance for several compelling reasons:

Restorative justice addresses the root causes of criminal behavior by involving offenders in the process of making amends and understanding the impact of their actions. This, in turn, reduces the likelihood of reoffending and leads to a safer society.

Traditional punitive approaches often fail to make offenders truly accountable for their actions. Restorative justice ensures that offenders face the consequences of their behavior, take responsibility, and actively work to repair the harm they've caused.

Victims have a central role in restorative justice, allowing them to express their feelings, needs, and the harm they've experienced. This empowers victims, supports their healing process, and addresses their psychological and emotional well-being.

Restorative justice encourages community participation, which strengthens the social fabric. Involving community members in the resolution process fosters a sense of ownership, solidarity, and collective responsibility for maintaining a safe and harmonious environment.

Restorative justice provides opportunities for personal growth and rehabilitation for offenders. This is crucial for addressing the underlying issues that may have contributed to their criminal behavior.

A fundamental shift in the criminal justice system is possible through the adoption of restorative practices. This involves courts, law enforcement, and correctional facilities embracing restorative justice principles and actively implementing them in their procedures.

Real-life case studies can demonstrate how the integration of restorative justice within the criminal justice system has reduced recidivism rates, healed communities, and promoted accountability. These examples highlight the effectiveness of restorative practices in achieving these outcomes.

Restorative justice is a system of justice that focuses on restoring relationships, healing harm, and addressing the needs of victims, offenders, and communities. It prioritizes a more humane and balanced approach to justice.

Punitive measures often perpetuate a cycle of harm, particularly within correctional facilities. Restorative justice aims to break this cycle by providing a space for individuals to repair harm and make amends.

Restorative justice empowers victims, offenders, and communities to be actively involved in the justice process. It gives them a voice and a role in shaping the resolution of the harm done, promoting a sense of justice and fairness.

Restorative justice has the potential to heal divisions within communities. By addressing conflicts and harm through open dialogue and reconciliation, it can promote unity and understanding.

The adoption of restorative justice principles can lead to a more just, compassionate, and reconciled society. It aligns with a vision of a criminal justice system that prioritizes the well-being of all stakeholders and the broader community.

Incorporating restorative justice into the criminal justice system can lead to profound changes, promoting healing, accountability, and unity. It shifts the focus from punitive measures to a more balanced and humane approach that supports rehabilitation, addresses the needs of victims, and reduces recidivism, ultimately creating a safer and more just society.

Educational transformation through restorative justice is a comprehensive approach to improving the school environment and addressing various issues. It aims to create a positive and inclusive learning environment while effectively addressing conflicts and promoting personal growth. Here's why it's crucial:

Restorative justice practices empower students and staff to address bullying incidents through dialogue, empathy, and understanding. This approach not only holds the offender accountable but also helps them understand the impact of their actions. It can prevent bullying and create a safer school environment.

Schools often face conflicts among students, teachers, and parents. Restorative justice provides a structured process for resolving conflicts by allowing individuals to express their feelings and concerns while working together to find mutually agreeable solutions.

Restorative circles, a key component of restorative justice in education, encourage open communication and active listening. They can be used for a variety of purposes, from addressing conflicts to building relationships and fostering a sense of community.

Restorative practices promote a sense of belonging and inclusion. When students and staff feel heard and respected, they are more likely to engage positively in their learning and working environments.

Restorative justice principles emphasize personal growth and rehabilitation. When students make amends and take responsibility for their actions, they have the opportunity to learn from their mistakes and develop as individuals.

Victims of harm within the school community need support and healing. Restorative justice provides them with a voice, allowing them to express their needs and feelings. It promotes their psychological and emotional well-being.

By addressing conflicts and fostering a sense of belonging, restorative justice helps create a safe, inclusive, and nurturing learning environment. This benefits students and staff alike, improving morale and overall well-being.

Restorative justice offers an alternative to punitive disciplinary measures, which often perpetuate a cycle of negative behavior. Instead, it focuses on teaching responsibility and accountability, helping students develop self-discipline.

Real-life case studies in educational institutions can showcase the positive impact of restorative practices on students, teachers, and the entire school community. These examples highlight how restorative justice principles transform schools into more empathetic, inclusive, and safe environments.

Educational transformation through restorative justice is about creating a supportive, respectful, and nurturing learning environment that addresses conflicts, supports personal growth, and fosters positive relationships among all members of the school community. It can significantly improve the overall educational experience for students and contribute to their long-term success.

Restorative practices offer a powerful framework for healing divided communities, and here's why they are particularly suited for this purpose:

Restorative justice places a strong emphasis on open and honest dialogue. In divided communities, where people may have opposing views and experiences, creating safe spaces for dialogue is essential. Restorative processes encourage individuals to listen to each other, share their perspectives, and seek mutual understanding.

In divided communities, there is often harm on both sides. Restorative practices require all parties to acknowledge the harm they've caused or experienced. This acknowledgment is a critical step in the healing process, as it validates the pain and experiences of everyone involved.

Through restorative processes like circles and conferences, individuals have the opportunity to hear one another's stories and experiences. This can lead to increased empathy, as people begin to understand the challenges, fears, and hopes of those on the other side of the division.

Restorative justice is fundamentally about reconciliation. It aims to repair harm and restore relationships. In divided communities, reconciliation is a vital step toward rebuilding trust and unity. When people can reconcile and move forward together, the community is more likely to heal.

Restorative justice processes hold individuals accountable for their actions, but in a way that is focused on personal growth and change rather than punitive measures. This accountability can lead to transformed behaviors and attitudes within the community.

Restorative justice practices support healing for individuals and the community as a whole. Participants can express their pain and emotions, and through the process, they often experience a sense of relief and closure.

Restorative practices are effective in transforming relationships. In divided communities, where relationships may be strained or broken, these practices provide a structured way to rebuild connections and foster a sense of belonging.

Restorative justice is not just about addressing past harm; it's also about preventing future conflicts. By creating spaces for understanding and communication, communities can work together to build a more inclusive and harmonious future.

Restorative practices can have a positive ripple effect on the overall community. As relationships are restored and unity is promoted, the community becomes a more supportive and inclusive place for everyone.

Case studies of divided communities that have successfully used restorative practices demonstrate the tangible benefits of this approach. These examples show how dialogue, empathy, and healing can mend divisions and promote unity.

In a world where divisions and conflicts are increasingly prevalent, restorative practices offer a path to healing and reconciliation. By fostering dialogue, understanding, and empathy, they can help divided communities come together, rebuild trust, and create a more inclusive and harmonious future.

Restorative justice can play a significant role in reconciliation on a national scale, especially in post-conflict societies. Here's how restorative justice principles can impact reconciliation at the national level:

Restorative justice principles encourage a comprehensive examination of historical wrongs and human rights abuses. This includes acknowledging past atrocities, such as genocides, mass killings, or systematic oppression, which have left deep scars on the national psyche.

Truth and reconciliation commissions, often influenced by restorative justice principles, provide a platform for uncovering the truth about past atrocities. These commissions investigate and document what occurred, creating an accurate historical record.

Restorative justice emphasizes accountability, but in a way that seeks transformation and healing rather than punitive measures. In national reconciliation efforts, this involves holding those responsible for past atrocities accountable, while also providing opportunities for them to acknowledge their actions and make amends.

Reconciliation on a national scale involves promoting healing for both survivors and the wider society. Restorative justice processes allow survivors and affected communities to share their experiences, express their pain, and seek acknowledgment from those responsible for the harm.

Trust is often shattered in the aftermath of conflict and atrocities. Restorative justice processes work to rebuild trust by creating spaces for dialogue, empathy, and understanding. This can lead to renewed trust among different groups within the nation.

Restorative justice principles encourage a focus on unity and the restoration of relationships. In divided post-conflict societies, this is essential for fostering national unity and cohesion. Reconciliation efforts aim to bring together communities that may have been on opposing sides of the conflict.

National reconciliation efforts that incorporate restorative justice also focus on preventing future conflicts. By addressing the root causes of the conflict and addressing grievances, these efforts aim to create a more stable and harmonious future.

Case studies from various post-conflict nations, such as South Africa with its Truth and Reconciliation Commission, demonstrate the real-world impact of restorative justice in national reconciliation. These examples show how addressing historical injustices through restorative processes can pave the way for national healing and unity.

Restorative justice principles, when applied in the context of truth and reconciliation commissions, play a vital role in addressing historical injustices, promoting accountability, and fostering national healing. By seeking the truth, holding individuals accountable, and focusing on healing and unity, restorative justice contributes to the broader process of reconciliation in post-conflict societies.

Empowering the marginalized through restorative justice principles is a powerful means to promote social justice and address systemic inequalities. Here's how these principles can have an impact:

Restorative justice goes beyond addressing individual actions and delves into the root causes of harm. It recognizes that systemic inequalities often contribute to marginalization and injustice. By acknowledging these inequalities, restorative justice can serve as a tool for addressing and rectifying them.

Restorative justice emphasizes community involvement and support. It provides marginalized communities with a platform to have their voices heard, share their concerns, and actively participate in decision-making processes. This empowers them to influence change in their communities.

Dialogue is a fundamental aspect of restorative justice. It provides an opportunity for marginalized individuals and communities to engage with those in positions of power, including authorities, institutions, and community leaders. These dialogues can lead to more inclusive policies and practices.

Restorative justice allows marginalized individuals to have their experiences and grievances acknowledged and validated. This recognition is essential for their healing and empowerment. It sends a powerful message that their voices matter.

Restorative justice can hold individuals, institutions, and structures accountable for their roles in perpetuating marginalization. By seeking reparations and redress, marginalized communities can address the harm done to them and work toward a more equitable future.

Restorative justice fosters empathy and understanding. When people from different backgrounds engage in dialogue and practice empathy, it can lead to a sense of solidarity and mutual support. This, in turn, can lead to collective action to dismantle oppressive structures.

Restorative justice practices can be applied in educational settings, promoting a more inclusive and equitable learning environment. By addressing issues such as bullying and discrimination, they create a space for students and educators to grow and thrive.

Restorative justice can facilitate the compensation and reparation of marginalized individuals who have been harmed. This not only addresses the harm but also helps to rectify systemic injustices.

Restorative justice principles can inform policy changes at various levels, including criminal justice, education, and social services. These changes can lead to more equitable and inclusive systems.

Real-life examples and stories from marginalized communities demonstrate the transformative power of restorative justice. These stories highlight how marginalized individuals have found their voices, gained redress, and contributed to dismantling oppressive systems.

Empowering the marginalized through restorative justice principles is a means to address systemic inequalities, promote social justice, and dismantle oppressive structures. These principles provide marginalized communities with opportunities for dialogue, acknowledgment, accountability, and policy change, ultimately fostering empowerment and equity.

Interfaith and interdisciplinary collaboration in the context of restorative justice is about bringing together individuals from diverse faith traditions, belief systems, academic fields, and professional backgrounds to work collectively in promoting justice, healing, and reconciliation. This collaboration is a powerful means of addressing complex societal issues and fostering positive change. Here's how it can make a difference:

Interfaith collaboration highlights shared values and ethical principles that are central to different faith traditions. Restorative justice principles, rooted in the teachings of Romans and embraced by various faith communities, provide a common ground for addressing issues related to harm, accountability, and healing.

Interdisciplinary collaboration involves individuals from various academic and professional fields. This diversity of expertise brings a broad perspective to complex issues. For example, legal experts, social workers, psychologists, and theologians can offer unique insights when working together on restorative justice initiatives.

Collaboration across faith traditions and academic disciplines fosters cultural sensitivity. It ensures that restorative justice practices are respectful of diverse cultural norms and practices, which is essential for promoting understanding and inclusion.

Diverse perspectives lead to innovative solutions. When individuals from different backgrounds come together to address a particular issue, they can create new approaches that may not have been considered otherwise.

Interfaith and interdisciplinary collaboration can lead to educational and awareness-building initiatives. This helps communities and society at large to understand the principles of restorative justice and their relevance in addressing contemporary challenges.

Collaborative efforts can lead to practical implementation of restorative justice principles. Communities may see the development of programs and initiatives that effectively apply these principles to real-world situations.

Case studies of successful collaborative efforts illustrate the positive change that can result from interfaith and interdisciplinary cooperation. These stories highlight how shared values and diverse expertise come together to address issues such as crime, conflict, and social divisions.

Collaborative groups can become advocates for policy changes that support restorative justice. By leveraging their collective influence, they can encourage legal and institutional reforms that align with restorative principles.

Interfaith and interdisciplinary collaboration inherently promotes inclusivity and equity. It recognizes the worth and dignity of every individual, regardless of their background, and strives for justice that is inclusive and equitable.

Collaborative efforts can foster strong community bonds. When individuals from diverse backgrounds come together to address common issues, it promotes unity, understanding, and a sense of shared purpose.

Interfaith and interdisciplinary collaboration in the context of restorative justice is a powerful means of promoting shared values, fostering understanding, and addressing complex societal challenges. Through diverse perspectives and expertise, these collaborative efforts create innovative solutions and advocate for policy changes that support restorative justice principles, ultimately contributing to positive change in communities and society.

Global inspiration in the context of restorative justice refers to the adoption and application of restorative justice principles in various parts of the world to address a wide range of local and global challenges. These examples demonstrate that restorative justice is not confined to one culture, region, or context but has universal relevance. Here are some illustrations of global inspiration:

1. South Africa's Truth and Reconciliation Commission: South Africa's Truth and Reconciliation Commission (TRC) is one of the most iconic examples of restorative justice on a national scale. The TRC aimed to address the historical injustices of apartheid by providing a platform for victims and perpetrators to share their stories and seek reconciliation. It served as an inspiration

for truth and reconciliation processes in other post-conflict societies.

2. Canada's Indigenous Healing Circles: In Canada, Indigenous communities have adopted the principles of restorative justice in the form of healing circles. These circles provide opportunities for dialogue, healing, and reconciliation, particularly in addressing historical injustices against Indigenous peoples. This approach has gained recognition and inspired similar initiatives globally.

3. Rwanda's Gacaca Courts: In the aftermath of the Rwandan genocide, the country established Gacaca courts as a form of community-based justice. These courts incorporated elements of restorative justice by encouraging perpetrators to confess their crimes and seek reconciliation with their victims. The Gacaca process served as an inspiration for transitional justice initiatives in other post-conflict regions.

4. Scandinavian Criminal Justice Systems: Countries like Norway, Sweden, and Finland have integrated restorative justice principles into their criminal justice systems. These systems focus on rehabilitation, reconciliation, and reintegration, rather than punitive measures. Their success in reducing recidivism rates has inspired criminal justice reforms in other parts of the world.

5. New Zealand's Restorative Justice Practices: New Zealand has widely embraced restorative justice practices, particularly within its youth justice system. These practices involve victims, offenders, and the community in finding solutions that repair harm and promote accountability. Other countries have

looked to New Zealand's approach as a model for juvenile justice reform.

6. Victims of Crime Support Groups: Support groups for victims of crime, which incorporate restorative justice principles, have emerged in various countries. These groups offer victims opportunities to share their experiences, find support, and seek healing. They draw inspiration from the idea that victims' voices should be heard and their needs addressed.

7. Community Policing Initiatives: Some communities around the world have adopted community policing models that emphasize restorative approaches to address conflicts and build trust between law enforcement and the community. These models have inspired innovative law enforcement practices in different regions.

8. Interfaith Peace and Reconciliation Initiatives: In regions marked by religious or ethnic conflicts, interfaith peace and reconciliation initiatives have embraced restorative justice principles. These efforts seek to bridge divides, promote dialogue, and facilitate reconciliation among different communities.

9. United Nations and International Efforts: The United Nations and international organizations have recognized the importance of restorative justice in various contexts, such as post-conflict peacebuilding and transitional justice. These global efforts acknowledge the universal relevance of restorative principles.

10. Non-Governmental Organizations: Numerous non-governmental organizations (NGOs) worldwide work to promote restorative justice principles in various areas, including criminal

justice, education, and conflict resolution. Their initiatives serve as global inspirations for grassroots restorative justice advocacy.

In summary, these global examples of restorative justice initiatives underscore the universal relevance of restorative principles in addressing a wide range of local and global challenges. They demonstrate the adaptability and effectiveness of restorative justice in various cultural, social, and political contexts and serve as inspirations for similar efforts around the world.

The vision for a restorative society is one where the principles of restorative justice are not merely an option but an integral way of life. It's a society that values healing over harm, understanding over judgment, and reconciliation over retribution. In this vision:

The default response to harm is healing. Instead of punitive measures that perpetuate cycles of violence and retribution, a restorative society prioritizes the recovery and well-being of all its members. Victims are supported, offenders are held accountable, and communities mend.

A restorative society holds individuals accountable for their actions and encourages them to take responsibility for their wrongdoing. It recognizes that accountability is not about punishment but about making amends and learning from one's mistakes.

Empathy and understanding are the cornerstones of this society. People actively listen to one another, seeking to understand each other's perspectives, experiences, and needs. This understanding fosters compassion and promotes unity.

Reconciliation is the ultimate goal, even in the face of deep conflicts. Communities strive to rebuild trust through dialogue and acknowledgment of past wrongs. They understand that true reconciliation takes time but is worth the effort.

A restorative society places a strong emphasis on preventing harm. It invests in conflict resolution skills, education, and community-building initiatives to proactively address potential conflicts before they escalate.

Restorative justice is woven into the educational system, teaching the next generation the principles of healing, accountability, and reconciliation. Young minds grow up with an understanding of restorative values.

Communities play an active role in addressing conflicts and promoting healing. Neighborhoods, schools, workplaces, and faith communities are equipped with the tools and training to facilitate dialogue and reconciliation.

The criminal justice system undergoes a fundamental shift. Prisons are transformed into places of rehabilitation, where offenders are given opportunities for personal growth and transformation. Recidivism rates decrease significantly.

The principles of restorative justice from the Book of Romans serve as a source of inspiration not only within communities but also on a global scale. Nations come together to address international conflicts with the values of reconciliation, understanding, and healing.

A restorative society embraces diversity, recognizing that every individual has inherent worth and dignity. It actively addresses systemic inequalities, working to dismantle oppressive structures.

Restorative practices are employed in various sectors, including family, schools, workplaces, and international diplomacy. Conflicts are resolved with the goal of healing and preserving relationships.

Interfaith and interdisciplinary dialogues thrive, promoting shared values of justice, healing, and reconciliation. Collaboration across diverse faiths, disciplines, and cultures enriches the society's capacity to address complex issues.

In this vision for a restorative society, the ongoing work of individuals, communities, and institutions is paramount. It's an acknowledgment that the transformation to a restorative way of life is a journey, requiring dedication and effort. But the potential for positive change in the lives of individuals, families, and communities is profound. It's a vision worth pursuing—one where reconciliation, understanding, and healing are at the heart of our shared human experience.

CHAPTER 15

CONCLUSION AND FUTURE DIRECTION

In conclusion, the exploration of restorative justice principles within the Christian context, particularly drawing from the teachings of the Apostle Paul in the Book of Romans, reveals a profound alignment between the values of Christianity and the tenets of restorative justice. This alignment underscores the deep theological underpinnings of reconciliation, healing, and accountability that are inherent in both Christian faith and restorative justice. The Book of Romans serves as a foundational scriptural basis for these principles, emphasizing the importance of healing and reconciliation over retribution, personal transformation and responsibility, and the inherent worth of every individual.

The future directions for the integration of restorative justice within the Christian context and society at large are promising. It is imperative for faith communities, churches, and Christian organizations to continue engaging in dialogue and education about restorative justice principles. Providing resources and training to clergy, church leaders, and members can empower them to actively practice and promote these principles within their congregations.

Additionally, the collaboration between different faith traditions and interfaith dialogue can further expand the reach of restorative justice. Shared values of healing, reconciliation, and justice are not limited to one faith but are universal. Engaging in conversations that transcend religious boundaries can foster a broader societal understanding of these principles.

In the criminal justice system, the integration of restorative practices should be a continued effort. Advocating for policy changes and legal frameworks that emphasize rehabilitation, healing, and accountability, inspired by the principles found in the Book of Romans, can lead to a fundamental shift in how society responds to wrongdoing. Moreover, the role of communities, schools, and workplaces in implementing restorative practices should be encouraged and supported.

Restorative justice has a significant role to play in addressing systemic inequalities and empowering marginalized communities. Its potential to dismantle oppressive structures and promote social justice cannot be understated. This means actively addressing issues related to race, socioeconomic disparities, and other forms of systemic discrimination.

Ultimately, the future of restorative justice lies in its continued expansion and adaptation. The ongoing development of training programs, educational initiatives, and public awareness campaigns can lead to its wider acceptance and integration into diverse aspects of society. As restorative justice principles continue to evolve, they offer a vision of a more compassionate, equitable, and reconciled world—a future well worth pursuing for individuals, communities, and societies.